Josiah

HOW A BOY KING TURNED HIS NATION BACK TO GOD.

J. Paul Taylor

Josiah: How a Boy King Turned His Nation Back to God

Trilogy Christian Publishers A Wholly Owned Subsidiary of Trinity Broadcasting Network

2442 Michelle Drive Tustin, CA 92780

Cover design by: Julianne Seely

For information about special discounts for bulk purchases, please contact Trilogy Christian Publishing.

Manufactured in the United States of America

10 9 8 7 6 5 4 3 2 1

Library of Congress Cataloging-in-Publication Data is available.

ISBN: 978-1-68556-220-5

E-ISBN: 978-1-68556-221-2

Dedication

While contemplating who I should dedicate this book to, I couldn't think of anyone better to dedicate it to than my wonderful family, who have experienced in their lives the very things that I have written about in the life of Josiah. I have watched each of you grow in your relationship with the Lord and have seen the Lord use each of you in His service. Your mother and I dedicated each of you to the Lord and to His service when you were born, and He has taken us at our word and used you not only here at home but around the world. We gladly relinquished our right for your presence with us now, knowing that we will be able to spend eternity with you in His presence.

Each of you: Karen Jordan, Renee' Seely, Dr. Jay Taylor, Julie Senff, Rev. John Taylor, and Rev. Elis Taylor, are special gifts from the Lord, and we have had the privilege of imparting into your lives the biblical principles which are now evident in each of your lives. God has granted to each of you a godly mate: Dr. Richard Jordan, Jeff Seely, Dr. Cheryl (Bye) Taylor, Rev. Gary Senff, Rev. Korie (Kuzina) Taylor, and Tracy (Barlean) Taylor, and given us fifteen wonderful grandchildren. And as of right now, twelve great-grandchildren. All of them being raised in God-honoring homes.

My prayer for you is taken from Paul's prayer for the church at Ephesus and Philippi,

> *I pray that the God of our Lord Jesus Christ, the Father of all glory, may give to you the spirit of wisdom and revelation in the knowledge of Him, the eyes of your understanding being enlightened; that you may know what is the hope of His calling,*

what are the riches of the glory of His inheritance in the saints, and what is the exceeding greatness of His power toward us who believe, ...being confident of this very thing, that He Who has begun a good work in you will complete it until the day Jesus Christ.

Ephesians 1:17–19, Philippians 1:6 (NKJV)

I want to give special attention to your mother (Dawn), who was a big part of who you all have become today. Dawn, I thank the Lord for the sixty-five years God has given us together and also for the impact you have had on each of our children. I love you!

We are the wealthiest couple in the world; all our children know the Lord as their Savior and are serving Him, and all our grandchildren and great-grandchildren are also living in godly homes, which will make their choice of serving the Lord very natural. We have no greater joy than to know that our children walk in the truth.

I will sign off as I do in all my correspondence,

Sincerely yours in the service of the King,

Dad

Acknowledgments

There have been many different people who have been a great influence in my life and have had a great impact on making me who I am today. I am grateful for my godly parents, who instructed me in the ways of the Lord. They faithfully took me to church, where I learned through Sunday school (while young) and youth group (as a teenager) the truths of the Bible. While growing up, there were a number of pastors, Sunday school teachers, and youth leaders who influenced my life and helped me during the time in my life when the decisions I made determined the course I was to take towards ministry.

I also want to thank Dr. Bruce Wilkinson (whom I have never personally met) for triggering this great curiosity in the life of King Josiah, king of Judah. His books have been a great inspiration for me in my studies of God's Word. The inspiration for the study in the life of King Josiah, however, came through his radio program on Josiah. I began to study his life. At that time, I was the pastor of Bethlehem Chapel in Ephrata, Washington. That study developed into a series of messages on his life that went for thirteen weeks. This book is the result of that study. I was so impacted by the life of King Josiah that I told my family, "If I ever write a book, it will be on the life of King Josiah."

I am the proud father of six wonderful children, all of whom are involved in ministry. Those who are not involved in full-time ministry are involved in various ministries in and through their church. After retirement from pastoral ministry, my youngest son, Elis, told me, "Dad, you have always wanted to write a book on the life of King Josiah, so now is the time to do it." With that, I began the task of putting into book form the study I had done.

I must acknowledge the help I received from two of my daughters-in-law, Dr. Cheryl Taylor, who took my manuscript and corrected the grammatical errors, and Tracy Taylor, who put it into manuscript form. I want to thank Tracy for her excitement in helping me bring this to completion and for her help with Trilogy Christian Publishing in getting it published. I also must acknowledge my granddaughter Julianne Seely for her skill as a graphic designer with the book cover.

I thank Rachel Hiatt and her team at Trilogy Christian Publishing for their thorough and professional work with editing and publishing. Their suggestions helped make this a better book.

I must give credit to the support my family has given me throughout this endeavor. I am truly a blessed man because all of our children are serving the Lord and raising our grandchildren in godly homes. To all of our children: Karen Jordan, Renee' Seely, Dr. Jay Taylor, Julie Senff, Rev. John Taylor, and Rev. Elis Taylor, and to our children's spouses Dr. Rick Jordan, Jeff Seely, Dr. Cheryl Taylor, Rev. Gary Senff, Korie Taylor, and Tracy Taylor I am deeply thankful for your support during the development of this book. And to my wife, Dawn, I am especially thankful. Your patience with me and unending help and encouragement have been a blessing. And thanks for the sixty-five years we have been together. *I love you!*

J. Paul Taylor

September 2021—Gig Harbor, Washington

Table of Contents

Introduction

Early in 1985, I was driving in my car and listening to a Christian radio station. On the program, I was listening to Dr. Bruce Wilkinson (founder and president of Walk Through the Bible Ministries) was speaking on the life of Josiah. I was so inspired by his presentation that I went home and began to study Josiah's life. From that study, this series of sermons on the life of Josiah came about.

The first thing that caught my attention was that Josiah had both a very ungodly grandfather and father. Since he was only eight years old when he became king of Judah, how did he get the reputation for being the godliest king that Judah had since David? Someone had to influence him for good, so how did that come about?

In my study of Josiah, it soon became evident that the growth in his life was a step at a time. Each step is outlined and begins a different phase in his relationship with God, which in turn leads to the next step. It was also evident that Josiah would not proceed to the next step if he hadn't taken the previous one.

The steps that Josiah took are also the same steps we take in our walk with God. These steps in the life of King Josiah show corresponding steps in our own lives, which bring us to the Lord and the development of our spiritual progression in Him.

These steps are presented here as chapters in his life story:

- Influence—Each of us has had someone who has influenced our lives for God.

- Inquiry—There came a time in Josiah's life when

he had to know the truth for himself.

- Purging—Once Josiah knew what the truth was, he acted accordingly and took decisive steps to clean up his life and nation.

- Commitment—Josiah committed himself completely to serving God.

- New Revelation—While restoring the temple, they found the Book of the Law, which revealed to him new truths about God.

- Humiliation—After hearing about God's judgment on sin, he humbled himself before the Lord.

- Proclamation—Since the warning of God's imminent wrath was true, he was obligated to share what he learned with the people.

- Return to Holiness—They returned to the worship of God and celebrated the Passover Feast.

James Smith has said, "The true value of a human life depends on its relationship to God." King Josiah had a rich and fulfilling life and relationship with God dramatically demonstrated by defining steps.

My prayer is that those who read this will see where they are in their relationship with God and cause them to press on to the next step in their journey with God.

CHAPTER ONE:
Heir to the Throne

Josiah was eight years old when he became king, and he reigned in Jerusalem thirty-one years. He did what was right in the eyes of the Lord and followed the ways of his father David, not turning aside to the right or the left.

2 Chronicles 34:1–2

Neither before nor after Josiah was there a king like him who turned to the Lord as he did—with all his heart and with all his soul and with all his strength, in accordance with all the Law of Moses.

2 Kings 23:25

Josiah's Name

The name "Josiah" means "May the Lord give" or "May the Lord support" or "May the Lord heal" (*Pictorial Encyclopedia of the Bible*, Merrill C. Tenney Ph. D. Vol 3, page 710, Zondervan Publishing House).

Date of His Reign and Life

Josiah became the sixteenth king of Judah. He reigned for thirty-one years in Jerusalem from 640–609/8 BC. The "people of the land" (2 Chronicles 33:25) enthroned him at the age of eight after the assassination of his father, Amon.

Josiah's Family Heritage

To get a better understanding of King Josiah, it is important to go back and look at his family history. Josiah's great grandfather, Hezekiah, was a godly man and leader, but both his father and his grandfather were wicked kings. It was because of their wickedness that God's wrath and judgment were administered upon Judah. Yet Josiah was a godly king who "did what was right in the eyes of the Lord and walked in the ways of his father David, not turning aside to the right or the left."

Josiah was the son of King Amon, the grandson of King Manasseh, and the great-grandson of King Hezekiah. He is also in the lineage of King David and, therefore, also in the lineage of Jesus.

Following are some of the highlights of the lives and reign of these three kings of Judah.

Josiah's Great-Grandfather, Hezekiah

Hezekiah's Godly Reign

Scripture: 2 Kings 18:1–8—The Righteous Reign of Hezekiah

> *In the third year of Hoshea son of Elah king of Israel, Hezekiah son of Ahaz king of Judah began to reign. He was twenty-five years old when he became king, and he reigned in Jerusalem twenty-nine years. His mother's name was Abijah daughter of Zechariah. He did what was right in the eyes of the Lord, just as his father David had done. He removed the high places, smashed the sacred stones and cut down the Asherah poles. He broke into pieces the bronze snake Moses had made, for up to that time the Israelites had been burning incense to it. (It was called Nehushtan.) Hezekiah trusted in the Lord, the God of Israel. There was none like him among all the kings of Judah, either before him or after him. He held fast to the Lord and did not stop following him; he kept the commands the Lord had given Moses. And the Lord was with him; he was successful in whatever he undertook.*
>
> **2 Kings 18:1–7**

The testimony that is said about Hezekiah is also said of his great-grandson, Josiah:

> *Hezekiah trusted in the Lord, the God of Israel. There was none like him among all the kings of Judah, either before or after him. He held fast to the Lord and did not cease to follow him; he kept the commands the Lord had given to Moses.*
>
> **2 Kings 18:5–6**

Neither before nor after Josiah was there a king like him who turned to the Lord as he did—with all his heart and with all his soul and with all his strength, in accordance with all the Law of Moses.

2 Kings 23:25

What a godly heritage Josiah had!

The Cleansing of the Temple

In the first month of the first year of his reign, he opened the doors of the temple of the Lord and repaired them. He brought in the priests and the Levites, assembled them in the square on the east and said, "Listen to me, Levites! Consecrate yourselves now and consecrate the temple of the Lord, the God of your ancestors. Remove all defilement from the sanctuary. Our parents were unfaithful; they did evil in the eyes of the Lord our God and forsook him. They turned their faces away from the Lord's dwelling place and turned their backs on him. ...Therefore, the anger of the Lord has fallen on Judah and Jerusalem; he has made them an object of dread and horror and scorn, as you can see with your own eyes. This is why our fathers have fallen by the sword and why our sons and daughters and our wives are in captivity. Now I intend to make a covenant with the Lord, the God of Israel, so that his fierce anger will turn away from us. My sons, do not be negligent now, for the Lord has chosen you to stand before him and serve him, to minister before him and to burn incense." Then the Levites set to work. ...When they had assembled their fellow Levites and consecrated themselves, they went in to purify the temple of the Lord, as the king had ordered, following the word of the Lord. The priests went into the sanctuary of

> *the Lord to purify it. ...Then they went in to King*
> *Hezekiah and reported: "We have purified the*
> *entire temple of the Lord."*
>
> **2 Chronicles 29:3–6, 8–12a, 15–16a, 18a**

Hezekiah made sure that he began his reign in the right way. He understood that without a right relationship with God, there could be no blessing of God upon his life and nation. Hezekiah started out by instructing the priests and Levites to perform their duties as and renew the worship of the Lord in accordance with the Law of Moses. He made sure they did the things that they were appointed to do.

Hezekiah demonstrates an important principle for us today. When those who have been called of the Lord to minister before Him will lead, then the people will follow and serve the Lord. The saying is true, "As the leaders follow the Lord, and as the priests follow the Lord, so also will the people follow the Lord." My prayer for us today is, "God, give us godly leaders who will faithfully follow You in doing the work of the ministry."

The Re-Consecration of the Temple

> *Early the next morning King Hezekiah gathered*
> *the city officials together and went up to the temple*
> *of the Lord. They brought seven bulls, seven rams,*
> *seven male lambs and seven male goats as a sin*
> *offering for the kingdom, for the sanctuary and*
> *for Judah. ...The priests then slaughtered the*
> *goats and presented their blood on the altar for*
> *a sin offering to atone for all Israel. ...When the*
> *offerings were finished, the king and everyone*
> *present with him knelt down and worshiped. ...So*
> *they sang praises with gladness and bowed down*

and worshiped. ...So the service of the temple of the Lord was reestablished. Hezekiah and all the people rejoiced at what God had brought about for his people, because it was done so quickly.

2 Chronicles 29:20–21, 24a, 29, 30b, 35b–36

What a time of rejoicing before the Lord. People are never as happy as they are when their leaders are right with God. This was a time of rejoicing for both the king and the people. "Hezekiah and all the people rejoiced at what God had brought about."

Keeping the Passover

Hezekiah sent word to all Israel and Judah and also wrote letters to Ephraim and Manasseh, inviting them to come to the temple of the Lord in Jerusalem and celebrate the Passover to the Lord, the God of Israel. ...The couriers went from town to town in Ephraim and Manasseh, as far as Zebulun, but the people scorned and ridiculed them. Nevertheless, some men from Asher, Manasseh and Zebulun humbled themselves and went to Jerusalem. Also in Judah the hand of God was on the people to give them unity of mind to carry out what the king and his officials had ordered, following the word of the Lord. A very large crowd of people assembled in Jerusalem to celebrate the Festival of Unleavened Bread in the second month. The Israelites who were present in Jerusalem celebrated the Festival of Unleavened Bread for seven days with great rejoicing, while the Levites and priests praised the Lord every day with resounding instruments dedicated to the Lord. For the seven days they ate their assigned portion and offered fellowship offerings and praised

*the Lord, the God of their ancestors. The whole
assembly then agreed to celebrate the festival
seven more days; so for another seven days they
celebrated joyfully. The entire assembly of Judah
rejoiced, along with the priests and Levites and
all who had assembled from Israel, including the
foreigners who had come from Israel and also
those who resided in Judah. There was great joy
in Jerusalem, for since the days of Solomon son of
David king of Israel there had been nothing like
this in Jerusalem. The priests and the Levites stood
to bless the people, and God heard them, for their
prayer reached heaven, his holy dwelling place.*

2 Chronicles 30:1, 10–13, 21, 22b–23, 25–27

This was such an important occasion that letters were sent
to those in the northern nation of Israel to invite them to come
and celebrate the Passover with them in Jerusalem. Some of
them were so far removed from the customs and worship of the
Lord that they just scoffed and ridiculed Hezekiah's attempt
at restoring the Passover Feast. But there was a remnant who
did have their roots deep in the things of God and who did
respond by going to Jerusalem and joining in.

The feast was so well accepted and enjoyed that the
people, after having celebrated for the seven days, asked to
continue on for another seven days of celebration. There had
not been a celebration like this one since the days of Solomon.
The celebration ended with the priests and Levites blessing
the people, and the chronicler noted, "And God heard them,
for their prayer reached heaven, his holy dwelling place."

The Nation of Israel Taken Captive

*In King Hezekiah's fourth year, which was the
seventh year of Hoshea son of Elah king of*

Israel, Shalmaneser king of Assyria marched against Samaria and laid siege to it. At the end of three years the Assyrians took it. So Samaria was captured in Hezekiah's sixth year, which was the ninth year of Hoshea king of Israel. The king of Assyria deported Israel to Assyria. ...This happened because they had not obeyed the Lord their God, but had violated his covenant—all that Moses the servant of the Lord commanded. They neither listened to the commands nor carried them out.

2 Kings 18:9–12

The recorder in 2 Kings noted, "This happened because they had not obeyed the Lord their God, but had violated His covenant." Somehow, despite the numerous warnings, Israel went blindly into judgment without a clue of their sin, and just between 300 and 400 years later, Judah followed along this same path and went into captivity in Babylon.

Hezekiah Rebels against the Assyrian Bondage

Scripture: 2 Kings 18:7b, "He rebelled against the king of Assyria and did not serve him."

Assyria's First Invasion of Judah

In the fourteenth year of King Hezekiah's reign, Sennacherib king of Assyria attacked all the fortified cities of Judah and captured them. So Hezekiah king of Judah sent this message to the king of Assyria at Lachish: "I have done wrong. Withdraw from me, and I will pay whatever you demand of me." The king of Assyria exacted from Hezekiah king of Judah three hundred talents of

silver and thirty talents of gold. So Hezekiah gave
him all the silver that was found in the temple of
the Lord and in the treasuries of the royal palace.

2 Kings 18:13–15

King Hezekiah rebelled against King Sennacherib and
tried to throw off the Assyrian yoke only to find that his nation
was in great peril, and he risked even more dangerous attacks
if he continued to rebel. Assyria was known for its cruel and
inhumane treatment of those they captured. At this time of the
invasion and capture of Israel, it is reported that over 27,000
people were deported from the region of Samaria.

Hezekiah's Sickness and Recovery

Scripture: 2 Kings 20:1–11

In those days Hezekiah became ill and was at the
point of death. The prophet Isaiah son of Amoz
went to him and said, "This is what the Lord says:
Put your house in order, because you are going to
die; you will not recover." Hezekiah turned his face
to the wall and prayed to the Lord, "Remember,
Lord, how I have walked before you faithfully and
with wholehearted devotion and have done what
is good in your eyes." And Hezekiah wept bitterly.
Before Isaiah had left the middle court, the word of
the Lord came to him: "Go back and tell Hezekiah,
the ruler of my people, 'This is what the Lord, the
God of your father David, says: I have heard your
prayer and seen your tears; I will heal you. On the
third day from now you will go up to the temple of
the Lord. I will add fifteen years to your life. And
I will deliver you and this city from the hand of

*the king of Assyria. I will defend this city for my
sake and for the sake of my servant David.'" Then
Isaiah said, "Prepare a poultice of figs." They did
so and applied it to the boil, and he recovered.*

2 Kings 20:1–7

This part of Hezekiah's history is very interesting. Here
was a godly king who walked in the ways of the Lord, and
when he got very sick and was about to die, he called on the
Lord, reminding the Lord of his faithfulness to Him during his
life. The Lord heard his prayer and granted him fifteen more
years. It is also ironic that during this time, he fathered the
next king of Judah, Manasseh, who became the most wicked
king to rule in Judah's history.

Hezekiah Entertains an Envoy from Babylon

*At that time Marduk-Baladan son of Baladan king
of Babylon sent Hezekiah letters and a gift, because
he had heard of Hezekiah's illness. Hezekiah
received the envoys and showed them all that was
in his storehouses—the silver, the gold, the spices
and the fine olive oil—his armory and everything
found among his treasures. There was nothing in
his palace or in all his kingdom that Hezekiah did
not show them. Then Isaiah the prophet went to
King Hezekiah and asked, "What did those men
say, and where did they come from?" "From a
distant land," Hezekiah replied. "They came from
Babylon." The prophet asked, "What did they see
in your palace?" "They saw everything in my
palace," Hezekiah said. "There is nothing among
my treasures that I did not show them." Then
Isaiah said to Hezekiah, "Hear the word of the
Lord: The time will surely come when everything*

*in your palace, and all that your predecessors
have stored up until this day, will be carried off
to Babylon. Nothing will be left, says the Lord.
And some of your descendants, your own flesh and
blood who will be born to you, will be taken away,
and they will become eunuchs in the palace of the
king of Babylon."*

2 Kings 20:12–18

During this time, the new coming world empire to rule—
Babylon—was having birth pains. They would become to
Judah what Assyria was to the northern nations of Israel.
And Isaiah prophesied that, eventually, they would be taken
captive to Babylon. This became a reality under the reign of
King Zedekiah, the last king of Judah and the third son of
Josiah.

King Hezekiah had great respect for Isaiah, the prophet.
He listened to him and took what the prophet said as the Word
of the Lord. Isaiah counseled him during most of his reign
in Judah. Hezekiah listened and obeyed Isaiah's instructions.
Isaiah was the prominent prophet during both Hezekiah's
reign and that of his son Manasseh. Manasseh, however,
didn't have the same respect for Isaiah that Hezekiah had. In
fact, his treatment of Isaiah was just the opposite of that of his
father. He beat, tortured, and persecuted Isaiah.

Assyria's Second Invasion of Judah

*Later, when Sennacherib king of Assyria and all
his forces were laying siege to Lachish, he sent
his officers to Jerusalem with this message for
Hezekiah king of Judah and for all the people of
Judah who were there: "This is what Sennacherib
king of Assyria says: On what are you basing your*

confidence, that you remain in Jerusalem under siege? When Hezekiah says, 'The Lord our God will save us from the hand of the king of Assyria,' he is misleading you, to let you die of hunger and thirst. Did not Hezekiah himself remove this god's high places and altars, saying to Judah and Jerusalem, 'You must worship before one altar and burn sacrifice on it'? "Do you not know what I and my predecessors have done to all the peoples of the other lands? Were the gods of those nations ever able to deliver their land from my hand? Who of all the gods of these nations that my predecessors destroyed has been able to save his people from me? How then can your god deliver you from my hand? Now do not let Hezekiah deceive you and mislead you like this. Do not believe him, for no god of any nation or kingdom had been able to deliver his people from my hand or the hand of my predecessors. How much less will your god deliver you from my hand!" ...Then they called out in Hebrew to the people of Jerusalem who were on the wall, to terrify them and make them afraid in order to capture the city.

2 Chronicles 32:9–15, 18

Sennacherib made the mistake of treating the God of Judah the same as all the other gods of the countries he had conquered. He also failed to realize that it was God who used him to bring judgment upon those wicked nations who had defied Him.

The King of Assyria Insults the God of Judah

Sennacherib's officers spoke further against the Lord God and against his servant Hezekiah. The king also wrote letters insulting the Lord, the God of Israel, saying this against him: "Just as the gods of the peoples of the other lands did not rescue their people from my hand, so the god of Hezekiah will not rescue his people from my hand." ...They spoke about the God of Jerusalem as they did about the gods of the other peoples of the world— the work of men's hands.

2 Chronicles 32:16–17, 19

In the first encounter, Sennacherib compared Judah's God to the gods of the other nations made by men's hands. But in this exchange, he spoke directly against the God of Judah.

King Hezekiah Spreads the Letter before the Lord

Hezekiah received the letter from the messenger and read it. Then he went up to the temple of the Lord and spread it out before the Lord. And Hezekiah prayed to the Lord: "Lord, the God of Israel, enthroned between the cherubim, you alone are God over all the kingdoms of the earth. You have made heaven and earth. Give ear, Lord, and hear; open your eyes, Lord, and see; listen to the words Sennacherib has sent to ridicule the living God. It is true, Lord, that the Assyrian kings have laid waste these nations and their lands. They have thrown their gods into the fire and destroyed them, for they were not gods but only wood and stone, fashioned by human hands. Now, Lord our God, deliver us from his hand, so that all the kingdoms of the earth may know that you alone, Lord, are God."

2 Kings 19:14–19

Hezekiah did the right thing here and laid the letter out before the Lord. Notice the main points of Hezekiah's prayer:

- He acknowledges that the Lord is the only true God.

- He asks the Lord to hear and see the insults that Sennacherib has made against Him.

- He acknowledges that the claims of Sennacherib were true in defeating the other nations, but only because they were really not gods at all but merely man-made objects of wood, stone, or precious metal.

- He implores the true God of heaven and earth to deliver them from Sennacherib's hand.

- Hezekiah asks that it be done so that all the kingdoms of the world will know that He alone is God.

God's Answer to Hezekiah through Isaiah

Then Isaiah son of Amoz sent a message to Hezekiah: "This is what the Lord, the God of Israel, says: I have heard your prayer concerning Sennacherib king of Assyria. This is the word the Lord has spoken against him: "...Who is it you have ridiculed and blasphemed? Against whom have you raised your voice and lifted your eyes in pride? Against the Holy One of Israel! By your messengers you have ridiculed the Lord."
..."Because you rage against me and because your insolence has reached my ears, I will put a hook in your nose and my bit in your mouth, and I will make you return by the way you came. ...

Therefore this is what the Lord says concerning the king of Assyria: 'He will not enter this city or shoot an arrow here. He will not come before it with shield or build a siege ramp against it. By the way that he came he will return; he will not enter this city, declares the Lord. I will defend this city and save it, for my sake and for the sake of David my servant.'"

2 Kings 19:20–23a, 28, 32–34

Through Isaiah, the prophet, God responded to Hezekiah's prayer. Here is the sum of what He said:

1. First of all, He assures Hezekiah that He has heard his prayer.

2. He confirms to Hezekiah that He truly is the one true God.

3. He confirms that Sennacherib truly did insult Him.

4. Because of the enemies' rage against the Lord, certain things are going to happen:

5. God will cause him to return to his own country of Assyria.

6. He will not shoot an arrow against the city.

7. Nor will he build a siege ramp against it.

8. God will defend the city for His name's sake and for the sake of David, His servant.

The Assyrians Defeated

That night the angel of the Lord went out and put to death a hundred and eighty-five thousand in the Assyrian camp. When the people got up the next morning—there were all the dead bodies! So Sennacherib king of Assyria broke camp and withdrew. He returned to Nineveh and stayed there.

2 Kings 19:35–36

Just as He had promised, God kept His word. During the night, the angel of the Lord killed 185,000 of the Assyrian army. With most of his fighting force now dead, Sennacherib could do nothing else but to retreat back to Nineveh.

King Sennacherib Murdered by His Own Sons

One day, while he was worshiping in the temple of his god Nisrok, his sons Adrammelek and Sharezer killed him down with the sword, and they escaped to the land of Ararat. And Esarhaddon his son succeeded him as king.

2 Kings 19:37

It is interesting that this king who challenged the God of Judah went back to his own country, and while worshiping in his own temple to the god Nisroch, was run through with the sword by his own sons and killed.

The Death of King Hezekiah

The other events of Hezekiah's reign and his acts of devotion are written in the vision of the prophet Isaiah son of Amoz in the book of the kings of Judah and Israel. Hezekiah rested with his ancestors and was buried on the hill where the tombs of David's descendants are. All Judah and the people of Jerusalem honored him when he died. And Manasseh his son succeeded him as king.

2 Chronicles 32:32–33

While Hezekiah was king, during the fifteen years following his illness, there was a change that occurred in his life. Before, he was humble and followed the Lord in every way; afterward, he was different than before and became very self-absorbed, only caring about what may happen to him:

1. He birthed a wicked son who followed him as king.

2. He entertained the emissaries from Babylonia.

3. When confronted by the prophet Isaiah, his response was, "'The word of the Lord you have spoken is good.' ...For he thought, 'Will there not be peace and security in my lifetime?'" (2 Kings 20:19). (He seemed to be only interested in his own peace and security.)

However, he was a well-loved king, and the people mourned his death.

The Wicked Reign of Manasseh

Manasseh was twelve years old when he became king, and he reigned in Jerusalem fifty-five years. ...He did evil in the eyes of the Lord, following the detestable practices of the nations the Lord had driven out before the Israelites. He rebuilt the high places his father Hezekiah had destroyed; he also erected altars to Baal and made an Asherah pole, as Ahab king of Israel had done. He bowed down to all the starry hosts and worshipped them. He built altars in the temple of the Lord, of which the Lord had said, "In Jerusalem I will put my Name." In the two courts of the temple of the Lord, he built altars to all the starry hosts. He sacrificed his own son in the fire, practiced divination, sought omens, and consulted mediums and spiritists. He did much evil in the eyes of the Lord, arousing his anger.

He took the carved Asherah pole he had made and put it in the temple, of which the Lord had said to David and to his son Solomon, "In this temple and in Jerusalem, which I have chosen out of all the tribes of Israel, I will put my Name forever. I will not again make the feet of the Israelites wander from the land I gave their ancestors, if only they will be careful to do everything I commanded them and will keep the whole Law that my servant Moses gave them." But the people did not listen. Manasseh led them astray, so that they did more evil than the nations the Lord had destroyed before the Israelites. The Lord said through his servants the prophets: "Manasseh king of Judah has committed these detestable sins. He has done more evil than the Amorites who preceded him and has led Judah into sin with his idols. Therefore this is what the Lord, the God of Israel, says: I am going to bring such disaster on Jerusalem and Judah that the ears of everyone who hears of it will tingle. I will stretch out over Jerusalem the measuring line used against Samaria and the plumb line used against the house of Ahab. I will wipe out Jerusalem as one wipes a dish, wiping it and turning it upside down. I will forsake the remnant of my inheritance and give them into the hands of enemies. They will be looted and plundered by all their enemies; they have done evil in my eyes and have aroused my anger from the day their ancestors came out of Egypt until this day." Moreover, Manasseh also shed so much innocent blood that he filled Jerusalem from end to end—besides the sin that he had caused Judah to commit, so that they did evil in the eyes of the Lord.

2 Kings 21:1–16

Manasseh was twelve years of age when he became king in Judah. He reigned for fifty-five years as king, the longest rule of any king in Judah, and died at age sixty-seven. During his reign, Manasseh was a vassal king under the rule of the Assyrians. Unfortunately, he was also the most wicked king to rule Judah. Some of the sins he committed:

- He followed the detestable practices of the nations the Lord had driven out before the Israelites.
- He bowed down to all the starry hosts and worshipped them.
- He built altars and put them in the temple of the Lord.
- He offered his own sons in sacrifice in the fire to Moloch.
- Practiced sorcery and divination and consulted mediums and spiritists.
- He persecuted the prophets who spoke against his reforms and heathen practices. (Tradition also says that Manasseh had Isaiah put to death by sawing him in half.)
- The testimony by the historian of 2 Kings says that "Manasseh led them astray, so that they did more evil than the nations the Lord had destroyed before the Israelites" (2 Kings 21:9b).

God said that He would use the same measuring line in dealing with Judah and their sin as He did against the northern country of Israel. He also said that His judgment will be so severe that "I am going to bring such disaster on Jerusalem and Judah that the ears of everyone who hears of it will tingle."

Manasseh's Captivity, Repentance, and Restoration

The Lord spoke to Manasseh and his people, but they paid no attention. So the Lord brought against them the army commanders of the king of Assyria, who took Manasseh prisoner, put a hook in his nose, bound him with bronze shackles and took him to Babylon. In his distress he sought the favor of the Lord his God and humbled himself greatly before the God of his ancestors. And when he prayed unto him, the Lord was moved by his entreaty and listened to his plea; so he brought him back to Jerusalem and to his kingdom. Then Manasseh knew that the Lord is God.

2 Chronicles 33:10–13

Assyria invaded Judah and took Manasseh captive to Babylon (Assyria used both Nineveh and Babylon as their capital cities). Manasseh humbled himself, and God heard him and restored him back to Jerusalem. Only then did Manasseh truly know that the Lord is God.

After His Restoration and Death

Afterward he rebuilt the outer wall of the City of David, west of the Gihon spring in the valley, as far as the entrance of the Fish Gate and encircling the hill of Ophel; he also made it much higher. He stationed military commanders in all the fortified cities in Judah. He got rid of the foreign gods and removed the image from the temple of the Lord, as well as all the altars he had built on the temple hill and in Jerusalem; and he threw them out of the city. Then he restored the altar of the Lord and sacrificed fellowship offerings and thank offerings on it, and told Judah to serve the Lord, the God of Israel. The people, however, continued to sacrifice at the high places, but only to the Lord their God.

2 Chronicles 33:14–17

And Manasseh rested with his fathers and was buried in his palace.

After repenting and returning to Jerusalem, he followed through and made some reforms in conformity with God's Word. Unfortunately, it was not as sincere as that of his father Hezekiah, "The people, however, continued to sacrifice at the high places, but only to the Lord their God."

King Amon's Reign and Death

Amon was twenty-two years old when he became king, and he reigned in Jerusalem two years. He did evil in the eyes of the Lord, as his father Manasseh had done. Amon worshiped and offered sacrifices to all the idols Manasseh had made. But unlike his father Manasseh, he did not humble himself before the Lord; Amon increased his guilt. Amon's officials conspired against him and assassinated him in his palace. Then the people of the land killed all who had plotted against King Amon, and they made Josiah his son king in his place.

2 Chronicles 33:21–25

Amon was twenty-two when he began his reign and reigned for two years and died at age twenty-four. He was also a vassal king under the Assyrians. The Bible says he did evil in the eyes of the Lord as his father had done.

Amon's father, Manasseh, was named after the son of Joseph, Manasseh (Manasseh means God has caused me to forget), but Amon was named after an Egyptian god. We are told three things about his character:

1. He did evil in the eyes of the Lord.

2. He worshiped the idols of his father.

3. By not humbling himself before God, he increased his wickedness and guilt.

His death was very tragic and cruel. His own servants murdered him in his own house. Amon died as he had lived, an unrepentant idolater in a very violent way.

The people didn't want anything to do with those who killed Amon; they put them to death for their crime and made Josiah king in his place.

Josiah's Mother, Jedidah

"Josiah was eight years old when he became king, and he reigned in Jerusalem thirty-one years. His mother's name was Jedidah the daughter of Adaiah; she was from Bozkath" (2 Kings 22:1).

We are not told anything about Josiah's mother other than she was the daughter of Adaiah from the city of Bozkath and her name, which means "Beloved of God," or "God's darling" (*Pictorial Encyclopedia of the Bible*, Merrill C. Tenney. Vol. 3, page 414, Zondervan Publishing House). It is very probable that she did have a godly background and influenced her son Josiah in the ways of the Lord. Josiah, while under her care, was likely encouraged to seek the Lord.

Josiah's Family

Josiah married Hamutal of Libnah, perhaps for diplomatic reasons (2 Kings 23:31) and Zebidah of Rumah (2 Kings 23:36).

Josiah had four sons by his two wives (1 Chronicles 3:15):

1. Zebidah, the daughter of Pedaiah of Rumah. Her sons were:
   a. Johanan, the firstborn (not mentioned anywhere else, may have died before Josiah)
   b. Eliakim (Jehoiakim), the second-born, succeeded Jehoahaz as king (2 Kings 23:34, 36; 2 Chronicles 36:4–5)
2. Hamutal, the daughter of Jeremiah of Libnah (not the prophet). Her sons were:
   a. Mattaniah (Zedekiah), the third born (succeeded Jehoiakim's son, Jehoiachin, as king) (2 Kings 24:17–18; 2 Chronicles 36:10–11)
   b. Shallum (Jehoahaz), the fourth born, succeeded his father, Josiah, as king (2 Kings 23:30–31; 2 Chronicles 36:1–2; Jeremiah 22:11)

Josiah is mentioned in Matthew's Gospel in the lineage of Jesus (Matthew 1:10–11): "Hezekiah the father of Manasseh, Manasseh the father of Amon, Amon the father of Josiah, and Josiah the father of Jeconiah and his brothers at the time of the exile to Babylon."

Josiah was only thirteen or fourteen when his first child was born, and the last one was born when he was eighteen. Josiah was the only king of Judah, or Israel, to have three sons succeed him as king. However, none of them followed in their father's footsteps. The Bible says of each of them, "He did that which was evil in the sight of the Lord" (2 Kings 23:32; 2 Kings 23:37; 2 Kings 24:19).

Political Environment: Assyrian Control

Assyria was the downfall of both the kingdoms of Israel and Judah. They took the northern country, Israel, captive in

721 BC, and they were the ones who really destroyed Judah as well. Judah had been pillaged and brought into a vassal state before they succumbed to the Babylonian kingdom. When Babylon came in and captured Judah in 606 BC, the destruction had already taken place by Assyria.

The Assyrians were, perhaps, the cruelest of the conquering nations.

The Assyrian policy was to deport conquered peoples to other lands, to destroy their sense of nationalism and make them more easily subject (and less likely to revolt). Assyrians were great warriors. Most nations then were robber nations. Assyrians seem to have been about the worst of them all. They built their state on the loot of other peoples. They practiced cruelty. They skinned their prisoners alive, or cut off their hands, feet, noses, ears, or put out their eyes, or pulled out their tongues, and made mounds of human skulls, all to inspire terror (*Halley's Bible Handbook*, page 209).

Early in Josiah's reign, the Assyrian grip on Palestine was already relaxing, but it was still politically and militarily in control of Judah. Josiah started as Assyria's vassal, at least in name, but with their weakening power and control, Josiah began to take cautious steps toward freedom. In 633/2 BC, Josiah, in turning back to the Lord (2 Chronicles 34:32), was turning away from an imposed dependency on Assyria and its gods. By 629/8 BC, Josiah was able to free the country of Assyrian as well as residual native cultic practices (2 Chronicles 34:3b–5). Not only was this carried out in Judah, but it also extended into the northern country of Israel (2 Chronicles 34:6–7). As Assyria weakened, Josiah found it increasingly easier to act independently so that when Josiah made the covenant with God and the people in 622 BC, it amounted to a formal defiance of the Assyrian deities and political control. However, as a vassal king under Assyria, it could have been assumed that his authority in Samaria and Megiddo was in the interest of Assyria. On the other hand, it may have been that Josiah hoped to restore the kingdom to the full scope of King David's kingdom.

Social Environment: The Rise of Godlessness

Manasseh led them [the people] astray, so that they did more evil than the nations the Lord had destroyed before the Israelites. The Lord said through his servants the prophets: "Manasseh king of Judah has committed these detestable sins. He has done more evil than the Amorites who preceded him and has led Judah into sin with his idols. ...Moreover, Manasseh also shed so much innocent blood that he filled Jerusalem from end to end—besides the sin that he had caused Judah to commit, so that they did evil in the eyes of the Lord."

2 Kings 21:9–11, 16

When Josiah came to power, he began his rule under the influence of both his father's reign and his grandfather's reign, Manasseh and Amon. Both of them were the most ruthless and wicked kings recorded in Judah's history. Sin and wickedness followed godless living and the worship of false gods. The corruption of Amon's reign, and the sin which he brazenly and boldly committed, were tell-tale signs of the coming wrath of a righteous God. Without the observance of the Jewish feasts and the God-ordained temple sacrifices and worship, the people followed the practices of the pagan rites and living that idol worship encourages. So the social life of the people was in following heathen practices and lifestyle.

To find out how severe his sin was, we have to go back to

his father Manasseh, because the Bible says,

> *He [Amon] followed completely the ways of his
> father, worshiping the idols his father worshiped,
> and bowing down to them. He forsook the Lord,
> the God of his ancestors, and did not walk in
> obedience to him.*

2 Kings 21:21–22

When Josiah came to the throne, Judah was under heavy tribute to Assyria. So taxation was very high, and the people were under great financial distress. Furthermore, because of the worship of other gods, which included very immoral conduct, there was a lack of restraint in their moral conduct. Crime was rampant within the city, and it was from the king on down to the average citizen of Jerusalem. It was another time in which each one "did that which was right in their own eyes." King Manasseh was so corrupt that the historian of 2 Kings says that he "shed so much innocent blood that he filled Jerusalem from end to end" (2 Kings 21:16). There was also an all-out war against the prophets of the Lord (more about that in the next section).

Those who were inclined to serve and worship God either were done away with, or they went into hiding. Godly people were hunted down, killed, and their property confiscated.

So when Josiah came to the throne, there were not very many godly and righteous people as its residence. This, of course, made his reforms even more difficult because it was "not popular" to follow God or to worship Him. And obviously, there were no temple sacrifices being observed. All of this makes it even more significant for Josiah to do what he did. And you can be sure that there was much opposition against his reforms. The fact that he did it with such confidence and boldness is outstanding. (God, give us leaders today who will be so brave and bold.)

Spiritual Environment: Spiritual Conditions under Manasseh

Scripture: 2 Kings 21:1–9, 16

Manasseh was twelve years old when he became king, and he reigned in Jerusalem fifty-five years. ...He did evil in the eyes of the Lord, following the detestable practices of the nations the Lord had driven out before the Israelites. He rebuilt the high places his father Hezekiah had destroyed; he also erected altars to Baal and made an Asherah pole, as Ahab king of Israel had done. He bowed down to all the starry hosts and worshipped them. He built altars in the temple of the Lord, of which the Lord had said, "In Jerusalem I will put my Name." In the two courts of the temple of the Lord, he built altars to all the starry hosts. He sacrificed his own son in the fire, practiced divination, sought omens, and consulted mediums and spiritists. He did much evil in the eyes of the Lord, arousing his anger. He took the carved Asherah pole he had made and put it in the temple, of which the Lord had said to David and to his son Solomon, "In this temple and in Jerusalem, which I have chosen out of all the tribes of Israel, I will put my Name forever. I will not again make the feet of the Israelites wander from the land I gave their ancestors, if only they will be careful to do everything I commanded them and will keep the whole Law that my servant Moses gave them." But the people did not listen. Manasseh led them astray, so that they did more evil than the nations the Lord had destroyed before the Israelites.

2 Kings 21:1–9

Since there were only two years between Manasseh's reign and Josiah's, the spiritual conditions under Amon had deteriorated considerably by the time Josiah came to power.

Alexander McClaren states in his exposition of Holy Scriptures (page 252) that:

> *[Manasseh] was smitten with a very delirium of idolatry and wallowed in any and every sort of false worship. No matter what strange god was presented, there were hospitality, an altar, and an offering for him. Baal, Moloch, 'the host of heaven' wizards, enchanters, anybody who pretended to have any sort of black art, all were welcome, and the more the better. No doubt, this eager acceptance of a miscellaneous multitude of deities was the natural result of being surrounded by the worshippers of these various gods.*

The scripture says that "Manasseh led them astray, so that they did more evil than the nations the Lord had destroyed before the Israelites."

The second thing Manasseh did to incur God's wrath was to disregard the prophetic warning given to him by God's prophets, mainly Isaiah. During this time, there were three prophets that were proclaiming God's Word and judgment on sin; Isaiah, Micah, and Nahum.

Josephus states that Manasseh,

> *By setting out from a contempt of God, he barbarously slew all the righteous men that were among the Hebrews; nor would he spare the prophets, for he everyday slew some of them, till Jerusalem was overflown with blood.*

> **Josephus,** *Antiquities of the Jews*
> **Book X, page 302**

Manasseh was the one who had Isaiah put to death, probably by sawing him in half.

God warned Judah that He would judge her the same as He did when He judged Israel.

Spiritual Conditions under Amon

Scripture: 2 Chronicles 33:21–25

> *Amon was twenty-two years old when he became king, and he reigned in Jerusalem two years. He did evil in the eyes of the Lord, as his father Manasseh had done. Amon worshiped and offered sacrifices to all the idols Manasseh had made. But unlike his father Manasseh, he did not humble himself before the Lord; Amon increased his guilt.*
>
> **2 Chronicles 33:21–23**

Under Manasseh and Amon, the people of Judah were well entrenched as idol worshipers. Amon reinstated all the idols and gods that his father had destroyed during his reformations, and this in only two years. This shows the depth and commitment that the people had to idolatry.

It seems as though when Judah retreated back to idol worship, they didn't do it gradually but reverted right back to where they were under the worst of Manasseh's reign. Had it not been for godly King Josiah, Judah would have likely been taken captive during Amon's reign or shortly thereafter.

The Restored Remnant of Israel

After the fall of the northern kingdom of Israel, there was a movement of godly people from Israel to Judah for specifically religious reasons. The first were Levites in the time of Rehoboam (2 Chronicles 11:14). In the time of Asa, others followed from Ephraim and Manasseh (2 Chronicles

15:9). Shortly after the Assyrian destruction of the northern kingdom, many from the devastated land resettled in Judah at Hezekiah's invitation (2 Chronicles 30). Presumably, not all who came for Hezekiah's great Passover remained, but archaeology has shown a sudden large increase in population in the region around Jerusalem at this time, and Chronicles specifically mentions "men of Israel ...who lived in the towns of Judah" (2 Chronicles 31:6). "The people of Manasseh, Ephraim and the entire remnant of Israel" joined with "the people of Judah and Benjamin and the inhabitants of Jerusalem" in restoring the temple in the days of Josiah (2 Chronicles 34:9). The kingdom of Judah had absorbed many from the northern kingdom over the years, from the time of the fall of Samaria and the northern kingdom.

Map of Josiah's Kingdom[1]

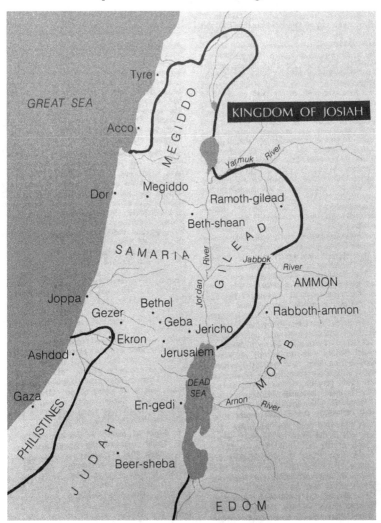

---

1   *Zondervan Pictorial Encyclopedia of the Bible*, Vol. 3, by Merrill C. Tenney, page 711

Principles for Life

1. Guide Your Children to Find God's Purpose for Their Lives.

It is the privilege and duty of every parent to guide their children in such a way as to make the will of God the greatest ambition of their lives.

The responsibility of the parents in training, instructing, and rearing their children in the things of God is perhaps the most important priority in their lives. Both Manasseh and Amon failed to do this, and the results of their lack of proper parenting affected the lives of generations to follow. Josiah didn't do any better than his father or grandfather.

In the case of Manasseh, his son turned out to be as wicked as he was, but in Amon's case, Josiah turned out to be a godly man in spite of his ungodly example. Unfortunately, he didn't pass on to his sons those godly principles.

2. Find God's Will for Your Life.

God has a plan and purpose for every child's life. To find it and live it out fully will mean blessing; to refuse or ignore it will mean failure.

Manasseh and Amon failed to find God's plan for their lives and were failures, both as men, fathers, and as kings. Hezekiah and Josiah realized God's plan for them, and they were successful both as men and as kings.

3. Make Wise Choices.

In the lives of these four kings, Hezekiah, Manasseh, Amon, and Josiah, we see the results of the choices that they each made. Hezekiah and Josiah were men who put God first in their lives and in their kingdom. Manasseh and Amon chose to serve the gods of the land and took Judah along with them into idolatry. Every person has the opportunity to choose to follow the Lord. The decision to serve the Lord or to go your own way is the individual's choice. The choices you make determine your destination. God will place in your life those who will influence you. Both Manasseh and Amon ignored godly influence and went their own way, but Hezekiah and Josiah chose to obey and serve the Lord.

4. **Live by God's Word.**

When we stand before God, we must answer to Him based on His Word. We are not going to be able to claim ignorance. We will be judged on what God has said. That is why it is important to instruct our children in the Word of God.

CHAPTER TWO:
Influence

Josiah was eight years old when he became king, and he reigned in Jerusalem thirty-one years. He did what was right in the eyes of the Lord and followed the ways of his father David, not turning aside to the right or the left.

2 Chronicles 34:1–2

Josiah was eight years old when he became king, and he reigned in Jerusalem thirty-one years. His mother's name was Jedidah daughter of Adaiah; she was from Bozkath. He did what was right in the eyes of the Lord and followed completely the ways of his father David, not turning aside to the right or to the left.

2 Kings 22:1–2

"Neither before nor after Josiah was there a king like him who turned to the Lord as he did—with

all his heart and with all his soul and with all his strength" (2 Kings 23:25).

Background

Manasseh, Josiah's grandfather, died after fifty-five years as king, and his son Amon became king at age twenty-two. After two years of an evil reign, his own officials killed him because of his wickedness. He was assassinated at age twenty-four and his son, Josiah, became king at age eight (2 Chronicles 33:24). Josiah was six when his grandfather died, and at the time of Josiah's birth, his father, Amon, was sixteen. Both of them were very ungodly. So, the obvious question is, with that kind of background in his family history, what caused Josiah to become a godly and righteous king?

God placed people in Josiah's life at this time to affect this result. So, who were they? To understand this question, we have to look at those who were the closest to Josiah and had influence in his life. That is the subject of this study. Several people were close to Josiah, and we will look at each of them in this study:

- Family Influence
  - His grandfather Manasseh, his father Amon, his mother Jedidah, his grandfather (on his mother's side) Adaiah
- Priestly Influence
  - Hilkiah, the High Priest
- Prophetic Influence
  - Nahum, Zephaniah, Jeremiah, Habakkuk, Huldah
- Administrators in His Cabinet
  - Ahikam son of Shaphan, Achor son of Micaiah,

Shaphan the secretary, Asaiah the king's attendant

We are also going to look at the importance of family influence, the influence of religious leaders in the lives of our children and conclude with the results of godly influence.

Family Influence

The Influence of His Grandfather, Manasseh

When Manasseh died, Josiah was only six years old. I am sure that there was a relationship that Manasseh had with his grandson, Josiah, but at that age, it probably didn't have much of an influence on his life in relation to establishing the character of his life. At that age, grandfathers are wonderful, fun-loving people who play with you.

But Manasseh did have an influence on his son Amon. Manasseh was forty-five years of age when Amon was born, and he died at age sixty-seven. So there were twenty-two years of influence that he had to instill in his son the importance of serving God. It is obvious that Manasseh did not do a very good job of accomplishing this task. We do not know how many years before his death that he reformed and turned back to serving God or how old Amon was at that time. Amon must have witnessed and observed his father recommit his life to God. And no doubt saw the results of that decision. But because of his youth—Amon was twenty-two when he became king—he, no doubt, surrounded himself with people of his own age and followed after their advice. This followed the same course that Rehoboam, son of Solomon, took when he became king, and with the same results; he followed the advice of the younger advisors.

The Influence of His Father Amon

Amon was twenty-two when he became king and reigned for just two years (he was assassinated at age twenty-four). And Josiah was eight years old when he became king, so his father, Amon, was only sixteen when Josiah was born.

One of the shortest histories of a king of Judah was that of Amon. Only seven verses in 2 Kings 21:19–26, and only five verses in 2 Chronicles 35:21–25 record his entire reign. During his life and reign, Amon was a very wicked man. Second Kings 21:20–22 sums up his life and reign,

> *He did evil in the eyes of the Lord as his father Manasseh had done. He followed completely the ways of his father, worshiping the idols his father had worshiped, and bowing down to them. He forsook the Lord, the God of his ancestors, and did not walk in obedience to him.*

Amon caused Judah to sin to the same degree as Manasseh had done before his reformation and that in just two years. Josiah was introduced to scenes of violence, idolatry, murder, outrage, and civil war by the time he was only eight years old and became king. Josiah did not have the input, counsel, discipline, or guidance of a godly father. This was the legacy that Amon left for his son Josiah. The fact that Josiah turned out as a godly man is most unusual and very rare. Fortunately, there were others in his life with godly influence that prevailed.

Just because a man is godly does not conclude that his children will be godly. Some of the godliest men were not good fathers. Eli, the priest, was a godly man, but his sons turned out to be evil (1 Samuel 2:22–25). Samuel, after having seen the example of Eli and his sons, also did not bring his sons up to fear the Lord (1 Samuel 8:1–5). David, also a godly man, did not raise his children up to follow his footsteps and serve the Lord. Adonijah, David's son who set himself up to succeed his father as king, was not disciplined. His father, David, "never rebuked him by asking, 'Why do you behave as you do?'" (1 Kings 1:6). Then, we come to Hezekiah, a godly man whose son Manasseh was a very ungodly and wicked man and king. All of these men failed to impart their character values into the lives of their sons.

Instilling godly principles into our child's life is a God-given responsibility that must be a priority for any father. Nothing else really matters if my children do not choose to follow the Lord. Proverbs says: "A fool spurns a parent's discipline, but whoever heeds correction shows prudence" (Proverbs 15:5). "Whoever heeds life-giving correction will be at home among the wise. Those who disregard discipline despise themselves, but the one who heeds correction gains understanding" (Proverbs 15:31–32).

The Influence of His Mother, Jedidah

> *"Josiah was eight years old when he began to reign, and he reigned in Jerusalem thirty-one years. His mother's name was Jedidah daughter of Adaiah; she was from Bozkath" (2 Kings 22:1).*

This passage is all we are told about Josiah's mother. But there is a lot of information in this scripture. We are told:

1. That her name was Jedidah, which means "God's darling." I do believe that her name is important to her influence in Josiah's life. She likely endeavored to make her son what she was called, "God's darling," and her effort did not go in vain.

2. That she was from the town of Bozkath, which was in Judah, west of the Dead Sea, near Lachish.

49

Lachish and Bozkath are listed in Joshua 15:39 as part of the inheritance of the tribe of Judah. Being from the tribe of Judah, she also became part of the lineage of David, therefore, also of Jesus.

The Influence of His Grandfather, Adaiah

"Josiah was eight years old when he began to reign, and he reigned in Jerusalem thirty-one years. His mother's name was Jedidah daughter of Adaiah; she was from Bozkath" (2 Kings 22:1).

Jedidah's father was Adaiah, which means "The honored of God." Both his mother and grandfather were godly people who could have had a great influence on his life. It is interesting to note the contrast: both his father and grandfather on his father's side were very ungodly, but on his mother's side, his mother and grandfather were godly people.

Some Conclusions about His Family Upbringing

Josiah became king at the age of eight, and it is obvious that at that age, he wasn't ready to understand all that was involved in being a godly king. There are some things that seem to be obvious about his training:

1. With the ungodly example that both his father and grandfather had in his life, he just didn't have the time to prepare for the responsibilities as a king, let alone a godly one.

2. His father, Amon, was only sixteen when his son, Josiah, was born, and as was the case for most royal families, his early training was left to

someone else.

3. It is reasonable to assume that he was still under adult supervision even while he was a boy king.

4. It is evident that those adults who were over him were godly.

5. They impacted his life for godly influence and training at this early age.

Priestly Influence

Hilkiah, the High Priest

Hilkiah, the high priest, appears to have had a good relationship with Josiah. Hilkiah worked very closely with Josiah in the collection of money for the repairs to the temple and then was also in charge of the oversight of the restoration work. Hilkiah was the one who found the "Book of the Law" while they were repairing the temple. He, in turn, brought it to Shaphan, the scribe who, in turn, took it to King Josiah (2 Kings 22:8). He was one of those chosen by King Josiah to go to the prophetess Huldah to inquire of the Lord for him concerning God's judgment on the nation because of Manasseh's sin. It is also very possible that as a young boy king, the high priest would take him under his wing and instruct him in the Word of God, similar to the way Eli took Samuel and brought him up to know God. It is apparent Josiah had received instruction as a young boy in the ways of the Lord, because according to the writer of Kings: "He did what was right in the eyes of the Lord, and followed completely the ways of his father David, not turning aside to the right or to the left" (2 Kings 22:2). And,

> *Neither before nor after Josiah was there a king like him who turned to the Lord as he did—with all his heart and with all his soul and with all his*

strength, in accordance with all the Law of Moses.

2 Kings 23:25

Hilkiah, the high priest, most likely had a great impact on the life of Josiah.

There are two names that appear to be those who had the most influence in his life at this age. They were his mother, Jedidah, and Hilkiah, the high priest. There is one other person who could also have had a godly influence in his life as well, his grandfather, Adaiah, on his mother's side. It was these that, I believe, impacted his life to make him the godly king that he was. In addition, several prophets were influential and likely impacted Josiah's life.

Prophetic Influence

The Influence of the Prophet Nahum

The prophet Nahum was called by God to proclaim the downfall of the Assyrian nation. His prophecy was probably between 625 and 612 BC when Assyria was in its prime. Assyria fell in 612 BC, and when Josiah died in 609 BC, Babylon was becoming the new world power. Nahum prophesied during the latter part of Manasseh's reign, during the two-year reign of Amon, and into the first part of Josiah's reign. He not only predicted the end of Assyria's world domination but the utter destruction of the nation. "The Lord has given a command concerning you, Nineveh; 'You will have no descendants to bear your name. ...I will prepare your grave, for you are vile'" (Nahum 1:14).

There is no evidence that Nahum and Josiah had a personal relationship, but Josiah would have known about his prophecy against Assyria. It is no doubt that this prophecy inspired Manasseh to rebel against Assyria and also caused

Josiah to take heart and look to the Lord for deliverance from Assyrian oppression.

The Influence of the Prophet Zephaniah

Zephaniah was, like Josiah, an ancestor of Hezekiah (Zephaniah by way of Cushi, Gedaliah, Amariah, and Hezekiah [Zephaniah 1:1]; Josiah by way of Amon, Manasseh, and Hezekiah). Zephaniah prophesied during the first part of Josiah's reign, probably before Josiah's reformations within the land (Josiah began to purge Judah in the twelfth year of his reign at age twenty). His prophecy was aimed at the degradation and ungodliness of Manasseh's and Amon's reigns. He warned about the coming destruction of the land to both Judah and its capital, Jerusalem. Josiah came to the throne in the year 641 BC and was twenty in the year 629 BC. Zephaniah was speaking out during that period, possibly during the last years of Manasseh's reign, the two years Amon's reign, and through the years of Josiah's reign until the time of the exile. Zephaniah was also a contemporary of the prophets Nahum, Jeremiah, and Habakkuk. Nahum's prophecies were directed against Assyria, whereas Zephaniah's prophecies were directed against Judah, Jerusalem, and the surrounding nations of Philistia, Moab, Ammon, Cush, and Assyria.

Zephaniah and Josiah must have had a personal relationship. The fact that they were relatives gave Zephaniah the opportunity to have input in his life, and no doubt, his prophecies had an impact on Josiah's life and his decision to serve the Lord.

The Influence of the Prophet Jeremiah

Jeremiah began his prophetic ministry during the thirteenth year of Josiah's reign (Jeremiah 1:1–2). Zephaniah identified himself with his royal lineage (Zephaniah 1:1), and Jeremiah identified himself with his priestly lineage. "The words of Jeremiah son of Hilkiah, one of the priests of Anathoth in the territory of Benjamin" (Jeremiah 1:1). Jeremiah's father, Hilkiah, was not the same as the High Priest Hilkiah under Josiah (There were a number of people named Hilkiah in the Old Testament, most of them associated with the priesthood). Jeremiah began his ministry halfway through Josiah's reign (640–609 BC) and continued through the reigns of Jehoahaz (609), Jehoiakim (609–598), and Zedekiah (597–586). It was a period of storm and stress when the doom of the entire nation—including Judah itself—was being sealed. In 612 BC, Assyria was defeated by the Babylonians, and in 605, the Egyptians were crushed at Carchemish on the Euphrates by Nebuchadnezzar. In the same year, he attacked Jerusalem and carried off Daniel and his three companions to Babylon. In 598/7, he attacked Jerusalem again, and Judah went into captivity for seventy years as prophesied by Jeremiah. Later, in 587/6, Jerusalem was captured and destroyed.

Jeremiah and Josiah, it seems, were very close and had an ongoing relationship. His input into Josiah's life and reign were, I believe, a contributing factor in the decisions that Josiah made in the period of his reformations. Jeremiah grieved when Josiah was killed fighting against Egypt and lamented Josiah's death. "Jeremiah composed laments for Josiah, and to this day all the men and female singers commemorate Josiah in the laments" (2 Chronicles 35:25).

The Influence of the Prophet Habakkuk

Little is known about Habakkuk except that he was a contemporary of Jeremiah. He anguished over the coming destruction of Judah and questioned God's justice in using such an evil empire to punish Judah, who was better than the Babylonians.

His prophetic ministry started toward the end of Josiah's reign and through the remaining kings of Judah, Jehoahaz, Jehoiakim, Jehoiachin, and Zedekiah. The time from the beginning of Josiah's reign (641 BC) until the captivity by Babylon was a period of about forty-two years. Like Jeremiah, Habakkuk probably lived to see the fulfillment of his prophecy when Jerusalem was attacked by the Babylonians in 597 BC. Jerusalem was finally destroyed in 588 BC.

It may have been possible that Josiah and Habakkuk knew each other; however, there is no evidence to support that.

The Influence of the Prophetess Huldah

What we know about Huldah is found in the passages in 2 Kings 22:14 and 2 Chronicles 34:22. She "was the wife of Shallum son of Tokhath [Tikvah], the son of Hasrah, keeper of the wardrobe. She lived in Jerusalem, in the New Quarter." Since she was the wife of the keeper of the wardrobe, she was no doubt of the tribe of Levi, who had the responsibility for the temple and its care. This included the inventory of the sacred items used in the temple service and would have been known to Hilkiah, the high priest. This relationship with Hilkiah was probably the reason that the delegation went to her, even though both Jeremiah and Zephaniah were actively prophesying at that time.

After Hilkiah, the high priest, found "the Book of the Law in the temple of the Lord" (2 Kings 22:8) and it was read to King Josiah, he tore his clothes and ordered a delegation to go and "inquire of the Lord for me and for the people and for all Judah about what is written in the book that has been found" (2 Kings 22:13).

Huldah confirmed that what was written was true and prophesied judgment and disaster on Jerusalem and its people, but not for Josiah, since the reading of the Law led to repentance and reformation in the land. For Josiah, she prophesied, "I will gather you to your ancestors, and you will be buried in peace. Your eyes will not see all the disaster I am going to bring on this place" (2 Kings 22:20). Josiah accepted that what she said was from the Lord and acted upon it accordingly.

It is interesting to note that with all the prophets who were prophesying during Josiah's reign, only Huldah is recorded as speaking directly into his life. It is also noteworthy that she is not mentioned again in Scripture, but she was in the right place at the right time and ready to speak what God would have her to say. The principle remains the same today; we never know how or when God will use us for His glory and honor.

Influence of Trusted Officials

Josiah's Cabinet Officials

There were four who had very close contact with King Josiah and were his personal advisors and confidants. They were: Ahikam, son of Shaphan; Achbor, son of Micaiah (he is called Abdon in 2 Kings); Shaphan, the secretary; and Asaiah, the king's attendant. These four were sent as a delegation from Josiah to Huldah, the prophetess, to inquire of the Lord about the words of the Law found in the temple.

Ahikam, Son of Shaphan

We know more about Ahikam than we do about the other three. In the reign of Jehoiakim, he protected Jeremiah from death. He was also the father of Gedaliah, whom Nebuchadnezzar made governor of the land after the destruction of Jerusalem (Jeremiah 26:24; 39:14; 40:5–41:18; 43:6).

Achbor, Son of Micah (Abdon in 2 Kings); Shaphan, the Secretary; Asaiah, the King's Attendant

These three were also part of the delegation that Josiah sent to Huldah. That is all that is said about them.

These four were trusted friends, aids, advisors, and counselors in the administration of Josiah. Josiah surrounded himself with people who were interested in the same goals as he was. You can tell about a person's character by those they surround themselves with as advisors. These men were in agreement with Josiah about the direction the nation should take and were supporters of the steps Josiah took to purge the land of heathen idols, practices, and altars introduced by his father and grandfather.

The Godly Influence of Family

You Can Make a Difference

The Christian home is God's plan for godly lives, homes, communities, and countries. If you have godly parents who have influenced you to serve the Lord, you indeed have been blessed. We have God's Word to support this: Proverbs 22:6 (NKJV), "Train up [instruct] a child in the way he should go, and when he is old he will not depart from it." *Never underestimate your godly influence in your child's life!* You have a greater impact than you realize. And we have the promise of God's Word: "Let us not become weary in doing good, for at the proper time we will reap a harvest if we do not give up" (Galatians 6:9). The eternal welfare and destiny of your children are at stake. Just as your godly parents have influenced your life so your godly influence will be just as effective in the lives of your children, and they, in turn, will influence the lives of your grandchildren.

Two Areas of Caution

1. Don't allow your children's complaining to cause you to compromise your standards, convictions, and principles. Hold tight; in the end, they will thank you for it. Remember, you are not your children's "best friend," you are their parent, so be a parent with conviction and determination. Best friend occurs after they become adults.

2. Don't succumb to their guilt trips. They will try to lay guilt trips on you to get what they want. There are two things that they will use on you:
    a. "Everybody's doing it." My answer was, "No, everybody's not doing it because you are not doing it."
    b. "You don't trust me." My answer was, "That's right! Trust is your responsibility to earn, so if I don't trust you, that is your fault; you have not proven to me that I can."

There Is No Substitute for Godly Praying Parents

Remember, for every victory in your child's Christian experience, it was won in prayer first by a godly parent. Hold your children up in prayer! Let them know that you are praying for them! And let them hear you praying for them! The following is a guide in praying for your children:

How to Pray for Your Children

1. Pray for Their Relationship with God:

    a. That they will turn from self and sin (2 Timothy 2:22).

    b. That they will turn toward the Lord to trust and follow Him (Proverbs 3:5–6).

    c. To know and serve Him (1 Chronicles 28:9).

2. Pray for Family Relationships:

    a. That there will be family unity (1 Peter 3:8–9).

    b. That they would be able to receive instruction and obey (Proverbs 1:8; Ephesians 6:1–2).

3. Pray for Their Schooling:

    a. That they would be teachable (Proverbs 4:13).

    b. That the principles of God's Word would be their criteria for discerning truth (John 8:32; Psalm 119:66, 99, 102).

4. Pray for Their Friendships:

    a. That they would not associate with evildoers (Proverbs 1:10, 15).

    b. That the Lord would provide "positive" friends (Proverbs 13:20, 27:17; Psalm 119:63; Hebrews 10:25).

5. Pray for Their Growth:

   a. That they will grow and develop physically (3 John 2; Luke 2:40).
   b. That they will grow and develop spiritually (3 John 4; 1 Timothy 4:12; 2 Peter 3:18).
   c. That they will grow and develop socially (Luke 2:52).
   d. That they will grow and develop mentally (Proverbs 2:1–6; 4:1, 5–8).
   e. That they will grow and develop emotionally (Proverbs 2:1, 9–11).

Get Involved in Your Child's Life

Don't let your life, work, or business interfere in your relationship with your child. God put him/her in your life to train them to know and serve Him. You have no greater calling or responsibility. Have clear and firm rules and guidelines for them. The following rules worked for us and probably would not work for everyone. However, make rules and guidelines that are pertinent and appropriate for you and your family, and then be consistent in enforcing them. Rules are only as effective as you enforce them. Don't give up; God is faithful! He will not fail you or your children!

The following are house rules and dating rules that my wife, Dawn, and I established for our children.

Household Rules:

1. No one could come over to the house without Mom or Dad being home.

2. Our children could not go to a friend's house without their mom or dad being there.

3. They could not stay overnight with people we

didn't know.

4. They had to be home Fridays by midnight and Saturdays by 11 p.m. (They must be their best for God on Sunday.)

5. They had the right to disagree with us, but they could not disobey us.

6. They must speak respectfully to parents.

7. They had the responsibility to keep their rooms clean and picked up.

8. They must respect the property of others.

9. Lying was not tolerated.

10. Drugs, alcohol, and tobacco were not tolerated (and never were a problem).

11. Each child had some household chores they were responsible for (dishes, help with meals, lawn, vacuuming, garbage, pets, and help with laundry and younger siblings).

12. Church attendance was mandatory for Sundays and mid-week (exceptions were considered on an individual basis and did not set precedence).

13. One meal a day was to be eaten together at the table as a family without the TV.

14. They must eat what is set before them *without complaining.*

15. If you have to smell, it's best to smell nice!

16. Allowances were paid when we could afford them.

Dating Rules:

1. Our children could only date other Christians.

2. They could not date until they were sixteen.

3. Boys dating our daughters had to get permission from Dad.

4. Our boys had to get permission from a parent of the girl they wanted to date.

5. They had to be home by midnight on Fridays and 11 p.m. Saturdays.

6. We had to know where they were going.

7. We had to know who they were going to be with.

8. Boys had to come to pick up our girls at the door. (They couldn't just honk for them.)

9. If curfew could not be met, it was the responsibility of our sons to call and let us know what was wrong and when they would be home.

10. If curfew could not be met while our girls were out, it was the responsibility of the boy to call and explain what happened and when they would be home.

11. If our daughters found themselves at a place or in a situation they were uncomfortable with, they were to call, and we would come and get them.

12. We never funded our sons' or daughters' dates. (It was their responsibility to come up with their own money for dating.)

13. We encouraged them to go to activities in a group. (Ball game, church outing, corner drive-in, school activity.)

14. Group dynamics are less stressful and more relaxed than one-on-one dating.

Be There for the Important Decisions

There are two decisions that your children will make that need your special attention, time, and prayer. The first one is their decision to give their life to Christ, and the second one is the decision they will make for a lifetime mate.

For a child growing up in a godly home where prayer and Bible reading are a daily part of their life, leading them to ask Christ into their life is a natural result of your home life.

It is natural for your children, as they grow older, to question what you believe and challenge you. Don't panic; you did the same thing with your parents. Just hold steady and pray. They must come to the place where they know Christ for themselves and the principles you have instilled in them they must own. You have trained them well, and the training will help them to come to the knowledge of the truth. *Remember, God is faithful!*

The second decision that is of the utmost importance is their decision for a lifetime mate. This is the time they need parental guidance. We let our children know that we would know who the right one is for them. We told them that we did not intend to choose their mate for them but that we would know who was right for them. It wasn't a matter of their choosing an unsaved person (they only dated others who were Christians) but one that would fulfill God's purpose for them. Our children were dedicated to the Lord as infants, and all of them felt God's call and hand upon their lives, so it was a matter of finding the right one. I am happy to say that (we have six children) we have three wonderful daughters-in-law and three great sons-in-law, all of them serving God where He has placed them.

There are two Bible stories that show how much parents impacted their child's life. The first one is the story of Moses (Exodus 2:1–10). Moses' mother took her son and raised him in a God-fearing way until he "grew older," and then Pharaoh's daughter had him. The impact of his mother's life and training caused Moses to choose to serve the Lord, choosing to be mistreated along with the people of God rather than enjoying the pleasures of Egypt (Hebrews 11:23–26).

The other is the story of Samuel's mother, Hannah. She raised her child, Samuel, to know God and then gave him to the Lord (1 Samuel 1:28). Samuel became a prophet of the Lord and led Israel for his entire lifetime. In both these stories, the fathers were very much in favor and part of what their wives were doing.

Samuel and Suzanna Wesley were God-fearing parents with nineteen children. Samuel was a preacher, and Suzanna was a prayer warrior. To find time alone with God, Suzanna would sit in her chair and lift her apron and put it overhead. The rule was that when Mother was behind her apron, she was not to be disturbed. Two of their nineteen children were John and Charles. John became the founder of the Methodist Church, and Charles wrote over 6,000 hymns. Both Samuel and Suzanna had a great influence on their children's lives.

I was very fortunate to have parents that knew the Lord. I am the second oldest of eleven children, eight boys and three girls. Our parents took us to church whenever the doors were open, and as a young child, I gave my life to Christ and dedicated myself to His service. I can remember hearing my mother praying for us downstairs as I lay in bed upstairs. Of the eleven children, seven have passed away, and the rest are all serving the Lord; some of us are in full-time ministry, the rest are involved in their local churches.

The Influence of the Church

The Influence of the Church Starts with the Parents

If you make the Lord an important and necessary part of your life, your children probably will too. Remember, it is your responsibility to so train your child in the ways of the Lord that they will automatically make the will of God the guiding force of their lives. Your home life, your personal life, and your family life should be so lived that your children will follow your example and make Him Lord of their lives. One of the ways to influence your child is to establish a time for "family devotions." They may not want it or even "goof off" during that time, but don't count the Holy Spirit short; He will do His work in their lives!

Should Church Attendance Be Mandatory?

I do not know how many I have spoken with that have made the fatal error of not making church attendance a priority for their children. It is your parental responsibility to teach and train them to know the Lord. You have the added help of having the influence of a godly church family to assist you. To say, "I will not force them to attend church and let them make their own decision for themselves when they are old enough" is one of the oldest, deceptive tricks of Satan. They do not have the maturity, nor the wisdom as a child, to make that decision. The only way they will do so is if they have been brought up in a godly atmosphere both at home and the church. You don't allow your children to decide whether they will attend school until they are old enough to make that decision, so why trust the decision about something as important as their spiritual training to them? Church attendance was, for our family, not ever talked about; it was part of our family practice. And being a pastor made no difference; it would have been the same if I were not.

You do not know who or what the Lord will use in the church to influence your child for the Lord; a Sunday school teacher, a youth leader, the pastor, or the pastor's spouse, other godly young people in the church. The truth is that we do not know who God will use to bring people to Himself. D. L. Moody, the great evangelist just prior to 1900, was won to Christ by his Sunday school teacher. The fact that your children are exposed to godly teaching of the Word, and the anointed preaching of biblical truth, will provide the opportunity for the Holy Spirit to work in their hearts and lives and draw them to Himself. There were many in our church family who had a great influence on the lives of our children. Today, as adults, they honor and cherish the impact they have had in their lives for God.

Do not underestimate the power of the Word of God spoken into the lives of your children. The apostle Paul wrote, "I am not ashamed of the gospel of Christ: for it is the power of God unto salvation" (Romans 1:16, KJV), and, "It pleased God by the foolishness of preaching to save them that believe" (1 Corinthians 1:21, KJV). Expose your children to the Word of God both at home and at church. One word of caution: Never punish your children by making them stay home from church or youth group! Use other means of discipline, such as taking away their social activities. The godly influence of your church in your child's life will have an impact for eternity.

The Results of Godly Influence

Josiah Did What Was Right in the Eyes of the Lord

The impact of the godly influence in Josiah's life was manifest in his determination to serve God. He didn't look for the approval of people, his peers, or his subjects. He wouldn't have gotten their approval anyway (they worshiped idols, the sun, moon, and stars, and would have rebelled if they could). I am sure that his actions caused an uproar and a lot of opposition in Jerusalem. It was popular to worship heathen gods, not the God of his fathers, Abraham, Isaac, and Jacob. It was not the most "politically correct" thing to do to tear down their idols to heathen gods, but he only sought to please the Lord.

The results of the godly influence in your children's life will come as you see your child grow and mature in the things of God and serve Him. When they make the principles that you have instilled in them part of their lives and character, then you will reap what you have diligently imparted to them. Don't give up hope! Raising children is hard, frustrating, time-consuming, tiring, exasperating, exhausting, strength-sapping work that demands everything you have. It takes everything you have and progresses only one day at a time. Don't panic; *God is faithful!* Draw your strength for Him.

He Did Not Turn Aside to the Right or the Left

Josiah was single-minded and was determined to please God. When you choose to please the Lord, you cannot please everyone else. You cannot serve God and another. God must be Lord of all, or He is not Lord at all. James says, "A double minded man is unstable in all his ways" (James 1:8, KJV). Josiah became a man obsessed with pleasing the Lord. The godly influence of those in his life helped to make him the man and king that he became.

What a wonderful statement that sums up his life,

Neither before nor after Josiah was there a king

like him who turned to the Lord as he did—with all his heart and with all his soul and with all his strength, in accordance with the Law of Moses.

2 Kings 23:25

The Influence of Your Life

Max Jukes, the atheist, lived a godless life. He married an ungodly girl. From that union, there were 310 who were paupers, 150 criminals, 7 were murderers, 100 were drunkards, and more than half of the women were prostitutes. His 540 descendants cost the state one-quarter of a million dollars.

Jonathan Edwards (1703–1758) lived at the same time as Max Jukes, but he married a godly girl. They had three sons and eight daughters. An investigation was made of the 1,394 descendants of Jonathan Edwards. From these descendants, 13 became college presidents, 65 college professors, 3 US senators, 30 judges, 100 lawyers, 60 physicians, 75 Army and Navy officers, 100 preachers and missionaries, 60 authors of prominence. The third Vice President of the US, Aaron Burr (born to their daughter Esther), served one term (1801–1805) under Thomas Jefferson. There were eighty who became public officials in other capacities, 295 college graduates, among whom were governors of states and ministers to foreign countries. His descendants did not cost the state a single penny.

Principles for Life

1. Recognize Those Who Influenced Your Life

All of us are where we are because of the influence of others in our lives. Those whom the Lord has allowed into your life have made you what you are today. Some have had an influence for good, and others have not, and we learn from both.

2. Maximize the Influence You Have in Other's Lives

God has placed you in the lives of others. How are you influencing them?

3. Appreciate the Godly Influence of Family

There is nothing that is more beneficial than having godly parents and family. God intended for the family to be the ones to impact their children for Him.

4. Thank God for the People He Has Strategically Placed in Your Life

God brings people into your life that will direct you and bring you to Himself. You never know what your life will help to produce in their life.

5. Assume They Will Be a Diverse Group

Just as there were family members, prophets, priests, and associates in Josiah's life, God will bring into your life those from different backgrounds into your life as well.

All are orchestrated by the Holy Spirit to guide you and bring you along in the knowledge and understanding of Him and His Word.

6. Allow the Holy Spirit to Do His Work

Let the Holy Spirit do His work in the lives of those God has brought into your life and influence. The Holy Spirit has come to draw men to Christ. Let Him do it. He is good at what He does!

7. Don't Give Up on Those God Has Put in Your Life to Influence

Don't just look at outward displays; God is at work inwardly. Bathe them in prayer and *trust Him*!

1. A Normal Life-Span Will Encompass Five Generations
    a. Your grandparents
    b. Your parents
    c. Your generation
    d. Your children's generation
    e. Your grandchildren
2. Remember, You Cannot Measure the Impact of Your Life within the Few Decades of Your Earthly Life Span

CHAPTER THREE:

Birth and Mission Foretold

Altar, altar! This is what the Lord says: "A son named Josiah will be born to the house of David. On you he will sacrifice the priests of the high places who make offerings here, and human bones will be burned on you."

1 Kings 13:2

Introduction

There are not very many in Scripture whose birth was foretold: Isaac (Genesis 17:15–19); Jacob and Esau (after Rebekah was pregnant) (Genesis 25:21–23); Samson (Judges 13:3–5); Samuel (1 Samuel 1:17) (though this may be questionable); Josiah (1 Kings 13:2); John the Baptist (Luke 1:11–13); and Jesus (Luke 1:26–31); these individuals were all foretold by prophets, priests, or angels.

This prophecy concerning the birth of Josiah occurred about 350 years before Josiah was born. Jeroboam became king in 975 BC, and Josiah became king in 640 BC. This prophecy by the "man of God" played an important part in the life of Josiah.

In this chapter, I want to look at the prophecy that foretold Josiah's birth by the "man of God" and the circumstances surrounding it. To do this, we must look at the period in Israel's history when Solomon's reign as king came to an end, and his son Rehoboam took his place and the subsequent division of the nation.

Israel Divided

Solomon's Reign and Death

Solomon was the wealthiest king recorded in the Bible. Second Chronicles 9:13–28 records his splendor, wealth, and influence among other nations, as well as his far-reaching economy.

The weight of the gold that Solomon received yearly was 666 talents (about twenty-five tons), not including the revenues brought in by merchants and traders. Also, all the kings of Arabia and the governors of the land brought gold and silver to Solomon.

King Solomon made two hundred shields of hammered gold; six hundred bekas (about seven and a half pounds) of hammered gold went into each shield. The king put them in the Palace of the Forest of Lebanon.

Then the king made a great throne inlaid with ivory and overlaid with pure gold. The throne had six steps, and a footstool of gold was attached to it. On both sides of the seat were armrests, with a lion standing beside each of them.

Twelve lions stood on the six steps, one at either end of each step. Nothing like it had ever been made for any kingdom. All King Solomon's goblets were gold, and all the household articles in the Palace of the Forest of Lebanon were pure gold. Nothing was made of silver because silver was considered of little value in Solomon's day. The king had a fleet of trading ships manned by Hiram's men. Once every three years, it returned, carrying gold, silver and ivory, and apes and baboons.

King Solomon was greater in riches and wisdom than all the other kings of the earth. All the kings of the earth sought an audience with Solomon to hear the wisdom God had put in his heart. Year after year, everyone who came brought a gift— articles of silver and gold, and robes, weapons and spices, and horses and mules.

Solomon had four thousand stalls for horses and chariots, and twelve thousand horses, which he kept in the chariot cities and also with him in Jerusalem. He ruled over all the kings from the River Euphrates to the land of the Philistines, as far as the border of Egypt. The king made silver as common in Jerusalem as stones, as cedar as plentiful as sycamore-fig trees in the foothills. Solomon's horses were imported from Egypt and from all other countries.

But his splendor and wealth were only part of the story. His reign put a very heavy tax burden upon the people.

Solomon also had twelve district governors over all Israel, who supplied provisions for the king and the royal household. Each one had to provide supplies for one month in the year. ...Solomon's daily provisions were thirty cors [about 185 bushels] of the finest flour and sixty cors [about 375 bushels] of meal, ten head of stall-fed cattle, twenty of pasture-fed cattle and a hundred sheep and goats, as well as deer, gazelles, roebucks and choice fowl. ...The district officers, each in his month, supplied provisions for King Solomon and all who came to the king's table. They saw to it that nothing was lacking. They also brought to the proper place their quotas of barley and straw for the chariot horses and the other horses.

1 Kings 4:7, 22–23, 27–28

This only accounts for the amount of food and supplies that it took to accommodate and feed those of the royal palace and staff for one day. It does not include the taxation to maintain his standing army, navy (1 Kings 9:26–28; 10:22), and his merchant marine corp. Nor does it account for those who worked within his government to oversee those he put to slavery. He conscripted those who were not Israelites but were part of his nation to serve as slaves, and those who were Israelites to serve in the military.

There were still people left from the Hittites, Amorites, Perizzites, Hivites and Jebusites (these people were not Israelites). Solomon conscripted the descendants of all people remaining in the land—whom the Israelites had not destroyed— to serve as slave labor, as it is to this day. But Solomon did not make slaves of the Israelites for his work; they were his fighting men, commanders of his captains, and commanders of his charioteers. They were also King Solomon's chief officials— two hundred and fifty officials supervising the men.

2 Chronicles 8:7–9

This ever-increasing tax burden was demanded and expected of the people, and it kept growing as his government and kingdom grew. But the people grew weary of the heavy burden he placed upon them, and when he died, they were looking for relief from this very heavy taxation.

Solomon Turns Away from Serving the Lord

There was one other very serious thing that occurred during Solomon's reign that played an important factor in the future of the kingdom. Solomon turned away from the Lord and began worshiping other gods.

King Solomon, however, loved many foreign women besides Pharaoh's daughter—Moabites, Ammonites, Edomites, Sidonians, and Hittites. They were from the nations about which the Lord had told the Israelites, "You must not intermarry with them, because they will surely turn your hearts after their gods." Nevertheless, Solomon held fast to them in love. He had seven hundred wives of royal birth and three hundred concubines, and his wives led him astray. As Solomon grew old, his wives turned his heart after other gods, and his heart was not fully devoted to the Lord his God, as the heart of David his father had been. He followed Ashtoreth the goddess of the Sidonians, and Molech the detestable god of the Ammonites. So Solomon did evil in the eyes of the Lord; he did not follow the Lord completely, as David his father had done. ...The Lord became angry with Solomon because his heart had turned away from the Lord, the God of Israel, who had appeared to him twice. Although he had forbidden Solomon to follow other gods, Solomon did not keep the Lord's command. So the Lord said to Solomon, "Since this is your attitude and you have not kept my covenant and my decrees, which I have commanded you, I will most certainly tear the kingdom away from you and

> *give it to one of your subordinates. Nevertheless,*
> *for the sake of David your father, I will not do it*
> *during your lifetime. I will tear it out of the hand*
> *of your son. Yet I will not tear the whole kingdom*
> *from him, but will give him one tribe for the sake*
> *of David my servant and for the sake of Jerusalem,*
> *which I have chosen."*
>
> **1 Kings 11:1–6, 9–13**

So, at the time Solomon died, there was quite a bit of unrest within the nation. The people were overburdened by taxation, the nation had turned away from serving the Lord, and God had already taken the kingdom away from Solomon's family and given them only a fraction of what it was under King David.

"And Solomon slept with his fathers, and was buried in the city of David his father: and Rehoboam his son reigned in his stead" (1 Kings 11:43, KJV).

The Israelites Appeal to King Rehoboam

When Rehoboam became king of Israel, the people appealed to him to lessen their tax burden.

> *Rehoboam went to Shechem, for all Israel had*
> *gone there to make him king. When Jeroboam son*
> *of Nebat heard this (he was still in Egypt, where he*
> *fled from King Solomon), he returned from Egypt.*
> *So they sent for Jeroboam, and he and the whole*
> *assembly of Israel went to Rehoboam and said*
> *to him: "Your father put a heavy yoke on us, but*
> *now lighten the harsh labor and the heavy yoke*
> *he put on us, and we will serve you." Rehoboam*
> *answered, "Go away for three days and then come*

back to me." So the people went away. Then King Rehoboam consulted the elders who had served his father Solomon during his lifetime. "How would you advise me to answer these people?" he asked. They replied, "If today you will be a servant to these people and serve them and give them a favorable answer, they will always be your servants." But Rehoboam rejected the advice the elders gave him and consulted the young men who had grown up with him and were serving him. He asked them, "What is your advice? How should we answer these people who say to me, 'Lighten the yoke your father put on us'?" The young men who had grown up with him replied, "These people have said to you, 'Your father put a heavy yoke on us, but make our yoke lighter.' Now tell them, 'My little finger is thicker than my father's waist. My father laid on you a heavy yoke; I will make it even heavier. My father scourged you with whips; I will scourge you with scorpions.'"

1 Kings 12:1–11

The request of the people was reasonable and would have truly brought the nation together under their new king in loyalty, purpose, and support. We're going to see from the life of Rehoboam that the decisions we make do have consequences. At the time we make them, many times, we do not realize the implications and consequences of what we are doing, but, as we shall see, time has a way of revealing to us the impact of what we have done.

Rehoboam Responds to the People's Request

Three days later Jeroboam and all the people returned to Rehoboam, as the king had said, "Come back to me in three days." The king answered the people harshly. Rejecting the advice given him by the elders, he followed the advice of the young men and said, "My father made your yoke heavy; I will make it even heavier. My father scourged you with whips; I will scourge you with scorpions." So the king did not listen to the people, for this turn of events was from the Lord, to fulfill the word the Lord had spoken to Jeroboam son of Nebat through Ahijah the Shilonite.

1 Kings 12:12–15

Instead of listening to the people and the elder counselors of his father, Solomon, Rehoboam rejected their counsel and adopted the counsel of the younger men he grew up with. And instead of lightening their tax load, he intended to increase it by many times over. This turn of events caused the people to revolt against King Rehoboam, and they broke off from Judah and made the nation of Israel. Only Judah and Benjamin remained with Rehoboam.

When all Israel saw that the king refused to listen to them, they answered the king: "What share do we have in David, what part in Jesse's son? To your tents, Israel! Look after your own house, David!" So the Israelites went home. But as for Israelites who were living in the towns of Judah, Rehoboam still ruled over them. King Rehoboam sent out Adoniram, who was in charge of forced labor, but all Israel stoned him to death. King Rehoboam, however, managed to get into his chariot and escape to Jerusalem. So Israel has been in rebellion against the house of David to this day.

1 Kings 12:16–19

God Had Prepared Jeroboam to Become King of Israel

Jeroboam, son of Nebat rebelled against the king. He was one of Solomon's officials, an Ephraimite from Zeredah, and his mother was a widow named Zeruah. ...Now Jeroboam was a man of standing, and when Solomon saw how well the young man did his work, he put him in charge of the whole labor force of the tribes of Joseph. About that time Jeroboam was going out of Jerusalem, and Ahijah the prophet of Shiloh met him on the way, wearing a new cloak. The two of them were alone out in the country, and Ahijah took hold of the new cloak he was wearing and tore it into twelve pieces. Then he said to Jeroboam, "Take ten pieces for yourself, for this is what the Lord, the God of Israel says: 'See I am going to tear the kingdom out of Solomon's hand and give you ten tribes. But for the sake of my servant David and the city of Jerusalem, which I have chosen out of all the tribes of Israel, he will have one tribe. I will do this because they have forsaken me and worshiped Ashtoreth the goddess of the Sidonians, Chemosh the god of the Moabites, and Molek the god of the Ammonites, and have not walked in obedience to me, nor done what is right in my eyes, nor kept my decrees and laws as David, Solomon's father did. ...I will take the kingdom from his son's hands and give you ten tribes. I will give one tribe to his son so that David my servant may always have a lamp before me in Jerusalem, the city where I chose to put my Name. However, as for you, I will take you, and you will rule over all that your heart desires; you will be king over Israel. If you do whatever I command you and walk in obedience to me and do what is right in my eyes by obeying my decrees and commands, as David my servant did, I will be with you. I will build you a dynasty as enduring as the one I built for David and will give Israel to you. I will humble David's descendants because of this, but not forever.'" Solomon tried to kill Jeroboam, but Jeroboam fled to Egypt, to Shishak the king, and stayed there until Solomon's death.

1 Kings 11:26, 28–33, 35–40

Jeroboam Is Installed as King of Israel

When all the Israelites heard that Jeroboam had returned, they sent and called him to the assembly and made him king over all Israel. Only the tribe of Judah remained loyal to the house of David.

1 Kings 12:20

Jeroboam Built Two Golden Calves for Israel to Worship

After Jeroboam became king, instead of relying on the Lord to establish his kingdom, he began to rationalize within his own understanding and caused all Israel to sin.

Jeroboam thought to himself, "The kingdom will now likely revert to the house of David. If these people go up to offer sacrifices at the temple of the Lord in Jerusalem, they will again give their allegiance to their lord, Rehoboam king of Judah. They will kill me and return to King Rehoboam. After seeking advice, the king made two golden calves. He said to the people, "It is too much for you to go up to Jerusalem. Here are your gods, Israel, who brought you up out of Egypt." One he set up in Bethel, and the other in Dan. And this thing became a sin; the people ...went even as far as Dan to worship the other. Jeroboam built

shrines on high places and appointed priests from
all sorts of people, even though they were not
Levites. He instituted a festival on the fifteenth day
of the eighth month, like the festival held in Judah,
and offered sacrifices on the altar. This he did in
Bethel, sacrificing to the calves he had made. And
at Bethel he also installed priests at the high places
he had made. On the fifteenth day of the eighth
month, a month of his own choosing, he offered
sacrifices on the altar he had built at Bethel. So he
instituted the festival for the Israelites and went up
to the altar to make offerings.

1 Kings 12:26–33

Instead of relying on the Lord to establish him as king, he
took it into his own hands to secure his kingdom. He failed
to remember the promise of the Lord through the prophet,
Ahijah, that it was God who was giving him the ten tribes.
Somehow, he failed to understand that what God promises He
is able to bring to pass. We don't have to depend on our own
devices.

The Obedient Prophet

The "Man of God" Sent to Bethel

By the word of the Lord a man of God came from
Judah to Bethel, as Jeroboam was standing by the
altar to make an offering. By the word of the Lord
He cried out against the altar: "Altar, altar! This
is what the Lord says: 'A son named Josiah will be
born to the house of David. On you he will sacrifice
the priests of the high places who now make
offerings here, and human bones will be burned
on you.'" That same day the man of God gave a
sign: "This is the sign the Lord has declared: The

altar will be split apart and the ashes on it will be poured out."

1 Kings 13:1–3

This prophet is only identified as a "man of God." We do not know his name, only where he came from, Judah. But there is a very clear outline of what he came to proclaim:

1. The prophecy the "man of God" proclaimed was against the altar Jeroboam had built.

2. A son of the lineage of David would be born in Judah, named Josiah.

3. He would sacrifice the priests of the high places on this altar.

4. He would burn the bones of the priests of Bethel who had died on this altar.

5. As a sign, the altar would split apart, and the ashes on the altar would be poured out.

Jeroboam Tries to Apprehend the Man of God

When King Jeroboam heard what the man of God cried out against the altar at Bethel, he stretched out his hand from the altar and said, "Seize him!" But the hand he stretched out toward the man shriveled up, so that he could not pull it back. Also, the altar was split apart and its ashes poured out according to the sign given by the man of God by the word of the Lord.

1 Kings 13:4–5

When Jeroboam heard the prophecy of the man of God, he stretched out his hand and ordered those at the altar to seize him. When Jeroboam ordered his apprehension, two things happened:

1. Jeroboam's arm shriveled up and

2. The altar split apart, and its ashes poured out just as the man of God had prophesied.

The Man of God Prays for Jeroboam

Jeroboam realized that he was dealing with more than just another man; he was dealing with the Lord. Immediately, he cried out to the man of God to pray for him.

> *Then the king said to the man of God, "Intercede with the Lord your God and pray for me that my hand may be restored." So the man of God interceded with the Lord, and the king's hand was restored and became as it was before. The king said to the man of God, "Come home with me for a meal, and I will give you a gift."*
>
> **1 Kings 13:6—7**

God's Instructions to the Man of God

> *But the man of God answered the king, "Even if you were to give me half your possessions, I would not go with you, nor would I eat bread or drink water here. For I was commanded by the word of the Lord: 'You must not eat bread or drink water or return by the way you came.'" So he took another road and did not return by the way he came to Bethel.*
>
> **1 Kings 13:8—10**

83

The instructions from the Lord were very clear as to what the man of God had to do. And he followed them to the letter. There was no wavering in his actions or words.

But then, things became confusing and costly for the man of God.

The Disobedient Prophet

An Interfering Old Prophet

There was an old prophet living in Bethel who was told about the man of God and his proclamation against the altar of Jeroboam. We are not told the name of this prophet; he is only identified as "an old prophet."

> *Now there was a certain old prophet living in Bethel, whose sons came and told him all that the man of God had done there that day. They also told their father what he said to the king. Their father asked them, "Which way did he go?" And his sons showed him which road the man of God from Judah had taken. So he said to his sons, "Saddle the donkey for me." And when they had saddled the donkey for him, he mounted it and rode after the man of God. He found him sitting under an oak tree and asked, "Are you the man of God who came from Judah?" "I am," he replied. So the prophet said to him, "Come home with me and eat." The man of God said, "I cannot turn back and go with you, nor can I eat bread or drink water with you in this place. I have been told by the word of the Lord: 'You must not eat bread or drink water there or return by the way you came.'"*

1 Kings 13:11–17

To this point, the man of God was in keeping with what the Lord had commanded him to do. But he was about to be tested beyond his better judgment, and he suffered the consequences for it.

The Old Prophet Deceives the Man of God

The old prophet answered, "I too am a prophet, as you are. And an angel said to me by the word of the Lord: 'Bring him back with you to your house so that he may eat bread and drink water.'" (But he was lying to him.) So the man of God returned with him and ate and drank in his house. While they were sitting at the table, the word of the Lord came to the old prophet who had brought him back. He cried out to the man of God who had come from Judah, "This is what the Lord says: 'You have defied the word of the Lord and have not kept the command the Lord your God gave you. You came back and ate bread and drank water in the place he told you not to eat or drink. Therefore your body will not be buried in the tomb of your ancestors.'" When the man of God had finished eating and drinking, the prophet who had brought him back saddled his donkey for him. As he went on his way, a lion met him on the road and killed him, and his body was left lying on the road, with both the donkey and the lion standing beside it. Some people who passed by saw the body lying there, with the lion standing beside the body, and they went and reported it in the city where the old prophet lived. When the old prophet who had brought him back from his journey heard of it, he said, "It is the man of God who defied the word of the Lord. The Lord has given him over to the lion, which has mauled him and killed him, as the word of the Lord has warned him."

1 Kings 13:18–26

It is vitally important that we obey the word of the Lord. If we obey, there are consequences, and if we disobey, there are consequences. The words of Samuel to Saul are very true, "To obey is better than sacrifice."

The Man of God Buried in the Old Prophet's Tomb

The prophet said to his sons, "Saddle the donkey for me," and they did so. Then he went out and found the body lying on the road, with the donkey and the lion standing beside it. The lion had neither eaten the body nor mauled the donkey. So the prophet picked up the body of the man of God, laid it on the donkey, and brought it back to his own city to mourn for him and bury him. Then he laid the body in his own tomb, and they mourned over him and said, "Alas, my brother." After burying him, he said to his sons, "When I die, bury me in the grave where the man of God is buried; lay my bones beside his bones. For the message he declared by the word of the Lord against the altar in Bethel and against all the shrines on the high places in the towns of Samaria will certainly come true."

1 Kings 13:27–32

The Old Prophet Went beyond His Calling

Those who profess special callings from God must not go beyond what the Lord has called them to do. When we go beyond what God has called us to, we not only do not speak for God, but we also affect those to whom we speak. God helps us to speak what He calls us to speak, but not to speak what He has not commanded us to speak. And Lord, help us to know the difference between the two.

The Man of God's Prophecy Came to Pass 350 Years Later

Later on, we will see how this prophecy came to pass in the life of Josiah some 350 years after it was given.

Principles for Life

1. God Plays No Favorites

No matter how much we follow and serve the Lord and are blessed, if we turn back, all the judgments of His Word will also come upon us as well. While Solomon was obedient, he was blessed, but when he turned away from the Lord, he also received His judgments.

2. The Consequences of Our Obedience Affects Others

When Solomon turned away from the Lord, it affected his whole realm, not just his life.

3. The Lust for Power and Greed Causes Us to Think Irrationally

Rehoboam's greed and sense of self-importance caused him to overreach in trying to establish himself as great as his father, Solomon. As a result, he lost his kingdom, and part of it was given to another.

4. We Must Obey to the Letter the Instructions of the Lord

Both Jeroboam and the man of God failed to obey the Word of the Lord and suffered for it.

5. We Must Trust God to Bring to Pass His Promise to Us

Jeroboam failed to believe that God would keep the people loyal to him and, trusting in his own wisdom, built altars in Bethel and Dan for worship.

Abraham's faith (Romans 4:21). Being fully persuaded that God had power to do what He had promised.

6. Servants of the Lord Are Held to a High Standard

The man of God that the Lord sent to Jeroboam was no doubt used to hearing from the Lord and following His instructions. He failed to comply implicitly and paid the consequences. We dare not follow another's "word from the Lord" for us without confirmation from the Lord Himself.

7. Not Everyone Who Says They Are a "Prophet of the Lord" Is

Just because someone says they are a prophet of the Lord doesn't mean we should blindly obey their word. God will confirm to your heart what His will is. Listen to the Lord for yourself. *He will confirm His Word!*

8. The Will of God Is Known in the Heart

Proverbs 3:5: "Trust in the Lord with all your heart and lean not on your own understanding."

God confirms His will to our hearts, not our heads. Our minds tend to argue against His word to us. But listen to your heart; that's where God speaks to us.

Both Rehoboam and Jeroboam relied on their rationale, and both were wrong.

9. God's Word Came to Pass in Spite of Human Failure

Rehoboam, Jeroboam, and the man of God all failed in their obedience to God's Word, but God still brought to pass the Word that He had promised. When God has declared something, we can be sure that He will bring it to pass!

10. God's Promises to You Will Come to Pass

Now to Him who is able to do immeasurably more than all we ask or imagine, according to his power that is at work within us, to him be glory in the church and in Christ Jesus throughout all generations, for ever and ever! Amen.

Ephesians 3:20–21

11. God Can and Will Reveal His Will to You Personally

Ephesians 5:15, 17: "Be very careful, then, how you live— not as unwise but as wise. ...Therefore, do not be foolish, but understand what the Lord's will is." He will reveal His will to you!

You do not need "a word from the Lord" from another. God will reveal to you His will for your life. If there is a word of prophecy for you, it will be one of confirmation.

12. God Will Confirm His Will to You

There are four ways God confirms His will to us:

1. The witness of circumstances.

2. The witness of the Word of God.

3. The witness of the Spirit in our hearts.

4. A word of prophecy/knowledge.

CHAPTER FOUR:
Inquiry

Josiah Begins to Inquire of the Lord

Josiah was eight years old when he became king, and he reigned in Jerusalem thirty-one years. He did what was right in the eyes of the Lord and followed the ways of his father David, not turning aside to the right or to the left. In the eighth year of his reign, while he was still young, he began to seek the God of his father David.

2 Chronicles 34:1—3

The Effects of Those Who Influenced Josiah's Life

Those Who Impacted and Influenced Josiah's Life

In chapter two, we looked at those who impacted Josiah's life while he was young:

1. His mother, Jedidah

2. High Priest Hilkiah

3. The prophets Nahum, Zephaniah, Jeremiah, Habakkuk, and Huldah

4. His Cabinet Ahikam, Achbor, Shaphan, and Asiah

All of these were great contributors to Josiah in his early formative years and influenced his life from age eight when he became king until age sixteen when he began to seek the God of his father, David. Those eight years were pivotal in his training and in his personal desire to follow the Lord. They played an important part in Josiah's personal life and in the direction he would take his kingdom.

A Time to Know Truth for Yourself

There comes a time in every life when the influence of godly parents, friends, counselors, the church, and relatives will come to an end. The time comes when each of us must know the truth for ourselves. The goal of every parent is to teach their child to come to the truth for themselves. As your children grow, their minds develop, and they begin to think for themselves. They come to that time when they must know for themselves. They must know if the things they were taught are right and true. They no longer are satisfied to accept or believe what they are taught just because Mom, Dad, a friend, or the church has said so. That is why it is so important for godly parents to instill in the lives of their children godly principles and character that will lead to them becoming godly men or women. To train your children in such a way that making the will of God the greatest goal and accomplishment of their lives is the epitome of successful parenting. And there will always be times in your life when you will need input from those you trust. The goal for the individual is to know the truth because of their personal pursuit of truth.

The Proverbs says it best: Proverbs 22:6, "Start children in the way they should go, and when they are old he will not turn from it."

Josiah Began to Seek God for Himself

We read that "in the eighth year of his reign, while he was still young, he began to seek the God of his father David" (2 Chronicles 34:3).

Josiah came to the throne at the age of eight, and at the age of sixteen, he began to seek God for himself. For eight years, from age eight to sixteen, he had the influence of those whom God placed in his life to guide and direct him in righteousness and the ways of his father, David. During those eight years, he was most likely under the tutelage of his mother, his grandfather, the high priest, and Zephaniah, the prophet. They did a good job of instructing this young, impressionable king because, at age sixteen, he began to seek God for himself. He came to that time in his life when he had to know for himself if what he was taught by those in his life was true and trustworthy.

This time of searching for truth lasted four years because the next event in his life is mentioned when he turned twenty years of age. Second Chronicles 34:3, "...In the twelfth year he began to purge Judah and Jerusalem." So, for four years he gave himself to seeking the Lord and coming to the truth for himself. It appears that during those four years, he came to the right conclusions because, at age twenty, he began to take a stand and action against the ungodly practices that had been the normal practices and way of life for the past seventy-seven years under Manasseh, Amon and the first twenty years of his reign.

Relate His Education to Today

During his first sixteen years, he was under tutelage by those in his life and kingdom. We could think of that as the equivalent of our school education today. Young people graduate from high school at about eighteen years of age. Then it's off to college for four years for their college education. Josiah spent four years of self-study (and he didn't have the benefit of online education) and came through about the same time as our young people graduate from college. The only difference between Josiah and young people today is that during his education, he was also the reigning king of Judah and had all the responsibilities of a nation. The fact that he came through with flying colors gives testimony to the fact that he sought truth in the right places.

The Time of Searching the Truth

The time of searching is also a time of questioning. It is the time when everything is up for questioning. Because there is a desire to know for sure, everything is questioned, from: "Who am I?" to "Why am I here?" and, "How do I know that is true?" It is normal for young people at this stage in their lives to question everything and everyone, even their parents. Parents, when your children question everything you say at this age, *don't panic*! Although they may sound rebellious, like they have rejected everything you have taught them, they have not. They are testing to see if what you say is worth taking a stand for. They may even question whether God really exists. But don't mistake honest questioning as rebellion or defiance of your authority and convictions. They may even challenge the very principles to which you hold strongly. Honest inquiry is healthy, and with the proper guidance, they will arrive at the truth for themselves. A healthy normal mind will want to know the truth.

During these years with our six children, my wife and I told them that they had the right to disagree with us but that they didn't have the right to disobey. We knew that, in a few years, they would, through learning and understanding, come to recognize that the positions of Mom and Dad were the right ones. They were just checking to see if the fences that we had put up were still in place, and the barriers for their protection were still there.

The Time of Influence Is Over

There comes a time in each child's life when, to a large degree, you have taught them everything you are going to teach them. To a great extent, everything you are going to impart to them you will have said by the time they are through school. Whatever you tell them, from then on, will be a repetition. So, trust that you've done a good job and that the principles you have imparted will guide them in their search for truth. Trust that the Lord will use the truths and the principles that you have instilled in them to help them come to the truth. This is the time to put into practice the promise of God's Word, "Be confident …that He who began a good work in them will carry it on to completion until the day of Christ Jesus" (Philippians 1:6). Trust that the Holy Spirit will do the work that Christ sent Him to do in the life of your child. Jesus said of the work and ministry of the Holy Spirit, "When he, the Spirit of truth, comes, he will guide you into all the truth" (John 16:13). As you cover your child with prayer, the Holy Spirit is faithful to do His part in guiding them to the truth and knowledge of Christ. And remember, you too went through this same phase in your life. Just as the Lord saw you through, He will also see your children through and bring them to Himself.

Go to the Right Source for Truth

Look for Truth in the Right Places

It is one thing to want to know the truth, but it is another thing to know where to look to find the truth. You cannot find truth if you look in all the wrong places. When you are looking for truth, you must go to the one who is truth, Jesus! He said: "I am the way the truth and the life. No one comes to the Father except through me" (John 14:6). Another way to read this passage is: "I am the Way, I am Truth, I am Life. No one comes to the truth except by Me" (paraphrased by the author). Since Jesus is truth, we must go to Him to find the true source of truth. Jesus said,

> *Ask and it will be given to you; seek and you will find; knock and the door will be opened to you. For everyone who asks receives; he who seeks finds; and to him who knocks, the door will be opened.*

> **Matthew 7:7—8**

That must be our experience, journey, and search for truth. When done this way, you will not be disappointed.

The Word of God gives us many examples of those who have both looked to the wrong sources as well as the right sources.

Solomon's Search for Truth

Solomon's testimony of his personal search for truth:

> *I said to myself, "Come now, I will test you with*

*pleasure to find out what is good." But that also
proved to be meaningless. "Laughter," I said, "is
madness. And what does pleasure accomplish?"
I tried cheering myself with wine, and embracing
folly—my mind still guiding me with wisdom. I
wanted to see what was good for people to do under
the heavens during the few days of their lives. I
undertook great projects: I built houses for myself
and planted vineyards. I made gardens and parks
and planted all kinds of fruit trees in them. I made
reservoirs to water groves of flourishing trees. I
bought male and female slaves and had other
slaves who were born in my house. I also owned
more herds and flocks than anyone in Jerusalem
before me. I amassed silver and gold for myself,
and the treasure of kings and provinces. I acquired
male and female singers, and a harem as well—the
delights of a man's heart. I became greater by far
than anyone in Jerusalem before me. In all this my
wisdom stayed with me. I denied myself nothing
my eyes desired; I refused my heart no pleasure.
My heart took delight in all my labor, and this was
the reward for all my toil. Yet when I surveyed all
that my hands had done and what I had toiled to
achieve, everything was meaningless, a chasing
after the wind; nothing was gained under the sun.
Then I turned my thoughts to consider wisdom, and
also madness and folly. What more can the king's
successor do than what has already been done? I
saw that wisdom is better than folly, just as light is
better than darkness. The wise have eyes in their
heads, while the fool walks in the darkness; but I
came to realize that the same fate overtakes them
both. Then I said to myself, "The fate of the fool
will overtake me also. What then do I gain by being
wise?" I said to myself, "This too is meaningless."*

For the wise man, like the fool, will not be long remembered; the days have already come when both have been forgotten. Like the fool, the wise man too must die! So I hated life, because the work that is done under the sun was grievous to me. All of it is meaningless, a chasing after the wind. I hated all the things I had toiled for under the sun, because I must leave them to the one who comes after me. And who knows whether that person will be wise or foolish? Yet they will have control over all the fruit of my toil into which I have poured my effort and skill under the sun. This too is meaningless. So my heart began to despair over all my toilsome labor under the sun. For a person may labor with wisdom, knowledge and skill, and then he must leave all they own to another who has not toiled for it. This too is meaningless and a great misfortune. What do people get for all the toil and anxious striving with which they labor under the sun? All their days their work is grief and pain; even at night their minds do not rest. This too is meaningless. A person can do nothing better than to eat and drink and find satisfaction in their own toil. This too, I see, is from the hand of God, for without him, who can eat or find enjoyment? To the person who pleases him, God gives wisdom, knowledge and happiness, but to the sinner he gives the task of gathering and storing up wealth to hand it over to the one who pleases God. This too is meaningless, a chasing after the wind.

Ecclesiastes 2:1–26

This is Solomon's conclusion in his search for truth:

Now all has been heard; here is the conclusion of the matter: Fear God and keep his commandments, for this is the duty of all mankind. For God will bring every deed into judgment, including every hidden thing, whether it is good or evil.

Ecclesiastes 12:13–14

The key to discovering the truth is to search in all the right places.

Warnings from Failures

Hear the warnings from those who looked in the wrong places:

1. Proverbs 12:15; "The way of fools seems right to them, but the wise listen to advice."

2. Proverbs 14:12; "There is a way that appears to be right, but in the end it leads to death."

3. Proverbs 21:2; "A person may think their own ways are right, but the Lord weighs the heart."

You will never find the truth if you look for it in drugs, alcohol, sex, or the pleasures of life. Truth is found in Christ. In your search for truth, go to the right source for it, and you will find it. Josiah's search was from the right source.

I have a friend who, while in college, was doing drugs. One night he was with some friends, and they all got high. While he was under the influence of drugs, he had this great illuminating thought. He knew that he would forget it by morning, so he wrote it down. In the morning, when he awoke, he remembered that he had had a great idea and that he had written it down. When he found the note and read it, he was astounded to read, "I am here because I am not anywhere else. I am not anywhere else because I am here!" When he realized what had happened, it was one of the turning points in his life, and he became a Christian and left his life of drugs for good.

Promises from God to Those Who Seek Him

1. God's promise to the Israelites: "If from there you seek the Lord your God, you will find him if you seek him with all your heart and with all your soul" (Deuteronomy 4:29).

2. God's promise to Solomon:

   And you, my son Solomon, acknowledge the God of your father, and serve him with wholehearted devotion and with a willing mind. ...If you seek Him, he will be found by you; but if you forsake him, he will reject you forever.

   1 Chronicles 28:9

3. God's promise to Asa, king of Judah:

   The Spirit of God came upon Azariah son of Oded. He went out to meet Asa and said to him, "Listen to me, Asa and all Judah and Benjamin. The Lord is with you when you are with him. If you seek him, he will be found by you, but if you forsake him, he will forsake you."

   2 Chronicles 15:1–2

4. The psalmist David's prayer to the Lord:

   You, God, are my God, earnestly I seek you; I thirst for you; my whole being longs for you, in a dry and parched land where there is no water. ...The king will rejoice in God; all who swear by God will glorify in him.

   Psalm 63:1, 11

Those who search for truth will find it and also the favor of the Lord. Their lives will be blessed, and they will walk in safety and peace.

Search for God in Your Youth

Josiah's Search for God Began in His Youth

The Bible says of Josiah, "In the eighth year of his reign, while he was still young, he began to seek the God of his father David" (2 Chronicles 34:3). He came to the throne at age eight, and at sixteen, he began his search for truth for himself. You cannot start too young in your quest for truth and an understanding and knowledge of God. And no matter how long you give yourself to knowing God, you will never, in your lifetime, come to know all there is to know about Him. But the greatest achievement is coming to have a personal relationship with Him. That is what Josiah came into—a personal relationship with the God of his father David.

His choice to serve God in his youth benefited him later in his life. Because of the sin and wickedness of his grandfather, Manasseh, the judgment of God was pronounced on the nation of Judah. But because Josiah gave himself to serve the Lord, the judgment of the Lord was postponed until after his death. Does serving God in your youth have its rewards? The answer is a resounding *yes*! And it is accompanied with no regrets.

Serve God from Your Youth

There are those who think that it is to their advantage to "do their own thing" while they are young and then in later life give themselves to the Lord. But that only leads to heartache and sorrow. Those who "sow their wild oats" while they are young must also accept the harvest of those seeds planted. *You will reap what you sow!* You cannot sow your wild oats all week long and then come to church on Sunday and pray for crop failure. You will reap the harvest.

Listen to God's Word:

1. Hosea 8:7, "They sow the wind, and reap the whirlwind."

2. Galatians 6:7–8,

   Be not deceived: God cannot be mocked. A man reaps what he sows. Whoever sows to please their flesh, from the flesh will reap destruction; whoever sows to please the Spirit, from the Spirit will reap eternal life.

3. Hosea 10:12,

   Sow righteousness for yourselves, reap the fruit of unfailing love, and break up your unplowed ground; for it is time to seek the Lord, until he comes and showers his righteousness on you.

4. Sow for yourselves righteousness, reap the fruit of unfailing love.

5. Listen to the testimony of King Josiah; while he was still young, he began to seek the God of his father David (2 Chronicles 34:3).

I have pastored for over forty-six years, and I don't know how many times I have heard people say, "Pastor, I wish that I had given my life to Christ while I was young." The heartache of wasted years and the regrets of not living for God catches up with you later in life.

What a difference there is for those who have served the Lord from their childhood. Go to the library and read the biographies of those who have lived for God. Find the stories of men and women who have lived their lives for the Lord. They have hundreds of stories of how faithful God was to them and how it does truly pay to serve the Lord. Men such as Billy Sunday, Mark Buntain, James Hudson Taylor, David

Livingstone, Praying Hyde, D. L. Moody, George Mueller, Gypsy Smith, C. T. Studd, Martin Luther, Charles Finney, Billy Graham, Goforth of China, Reese Howels; and women such as Fanny Crosby, Corrie Ten Boom, Gracie Burnham, Rachel Saint, Joni Erickson, and Elisabeth Elliot. These share stories of God's faithfulness and the tremendous hope they have in being reunited with their loved ones and with the Lord.

Then there are those who didn't serve the Lord and the regrets they have, the sorrow and the heartache. Mostly because they didn't raise their children to know Christ and the sorrow they have in knowing that they won't make it to heaven and be reunited with them, they truly experience the heartache of reaping the whirlwind. Both of the options have eternal consequences. One for eternity with the Lord, the other eternity without the Lord. It's your choice!

God Has a Plan for Your Life

Many of those used by the Lord were called into His service as children. Listen to His voice while you are young. You see, God does have a plan for you, and it is a plan free from heartache and sorrow. That isn't to say that they didn't have difficult times, but they had the comforting presence of the Lord with them.

In the Old Testament, we have a list of people who were called as children by the Lord: Isaac, Jacob, Joseph, Moses, David, Josiah; and in the New Testament, there was John the Baptist, and the twelve disciples were all young men when chosen by the Lord. Then when you turn to Hebrews, chapter eleven, you get the list of those who served God in faith and received the promise of faithfulness.

Listen to the Word of the Lord for you,

> *"I know the plans I have for you," declares the*
> *Lord, "plans to prosper you and not to harm you,*
> *plans to give you hope and a future. Then you will*
> *call on me and come and pray to me, and I will*
> *listen to you. You will seek me and find me when*
> *you seek me with all your heart. I will be found by*
> *you," declares the Lord.*

Jeremiah 29:11—14

Yes, God does have a plan for your life. One that is exciting, fulfilling, adventurous, rewarding, and satisfying.

Contrast between Rehoboam and Josiah

When Solomon died, Rehoboam became heir to the throne. When the people approached him with a request to lighten their load, he turned for advice to young men who were his peers who advised him wrongly, and, as a result, God took the kingdom away from him and gave the northern ten tribes to Jeroboam.

Josiah, on the other hand, turned for his guidance and instructions to the Lord and the Lord restored to him most of the territory that was lost under Rehoboam (see the map of the kingdom of Josiah). Under his reign, he ruled over the land that was under kings David and Solomon.

Principles for Life

1. **There Comes a Time in Every Life When Your Own Integrity Demands That You Know What Is True for Yourself**

Your own sense of self-worth needs to know what you believe

and why you believe it.

2. To Arrive at Truth, You Must Get the Right Information

You must seek out the right sources in your search for truth.

3. To Arrive at Truth, You Must Surround Yourself with People of Integrity

Find people who will guide you to come to the right conclusions.

4. Jesus Christ Is Truth

Immerse yourself in a relationship with the one who is the truth.

5. The Word of God Is the Prime Source for Truth

Let the Word of God infiltrate your life and spirit. The Holy Spirit will illuminate God's Word to you.

6. Give Yourself to Seek God While You Are Young

Let the Lord mold you into His likeness; then, you will have something to live for.

7. God's Plan for Your Life Is Greater Than Anything You Could Ever Devise for Yourself

His plans for your life will astound you and all who observe your life.

Hang on and enjoy the ride!

CHAPTER FIVE:
Purging

Josiah Purges the Land and the Temple

In his twelfth year he began to purge Judah and Jerusalem of high places, Asherah poles, and idols. Under his direction the altars of the Baals were torn down; he cut to pieces the incense altars that were above them, and smashed the Asherah poles and the idols. These he broke to pieces and scattered over the graves of those who had sacrificed to them. He burned the bones of the priests on their altars, and so he purged Judah and Jerusalem. In the towns of Manasseh, Ephraim and Simeon, as far as Naphtali, and in the ruins around them, he tore down the altars and the Asherah poles and crushed the idols to powder and cut to pieces all the incense altars throughout Israel. Then he went back to Jerusalem. ...Neither before nor after king

> *Josiah was there a king like him who turned to the*
> *Lord as he did—with all his heart and with all his*
> *soul and with all his strength.*

2 Chronicles 34:3b–7; 2 Kings 23:25

The Impact of Truth

Truth Will Change Who You Are

There comes that point in your life, after coming into truth, that you must act upon what you have learned. You cannot come to understand something to be true without it having an impact on the way you live. This is more than just giving mental assent to what you have learned. To come to know something and just give mental assent to it without it having any effect or change in your life is the same as not believing it in the first place or accepting it as truth. It is impossible to know the truth and not have it change your life. Once you have discovered the truth, you must act upon it from that point on. Jesus said, "If you hold to my teaching, you are really my disciples. Then you will know the truth, and the truth will set you free" (John 8:31–32).

Let me illustrate. Once you know that one plus one equals two, you cannot add it to come out any other way. You are responsible for that knowledge, and you must act accordingly. I must always add it to be two. And once we come to the knowledge of who Jesus is, we must act accordingly upon that knowledge. In fact, for us to live in society and become productive members of society, we must act according to the truth. All of our actions and decisions are based on truth as we know it. If we are mistaken about a truth and act accordingly, we end up in a mess and pay the consequences. But when I know something to be true, I am free to act in confidence because truth cannot fail.

Responsibility and truth go hand in hand. A child growing up doesn't have many responsibilities, but as he begins to learn, he is given more responsibilities and is held accountable for them. Truth literally changes who you are and the way you do things.

Josiah Acted According to His Newfound Knowledge

Josiah gave himself to seeking God when he was sixteen, and for four years, he immersed himself in his own theological seminary. He gave himself to know God. What he learned changed his way of life and the way he ruled his nation. It so changed his life that he is known as the godly king who sought the Lord, "Neither before nor after king Josiah was there a king like him who turned to the Lord as he did—with all his heart and with all his soul and with all his strength" (2 Kings 23:25).

Both Judah and Jerusalem were idolatrous. They had lived with idolatry under Manasseh for fifty-five years and under Amon for two years. Then, add to that the twelve years under Josiah before He came to the knowledge of the truth, and you have sixty-nine years of continuous idolatry. That is nearly three generations.

Once Josiah came to realize that God says, "You shall have no other gods before me. You shall not make for yourself an image in any form. ... You shall not bow down to them or worship them" (Deuteronomy 5:7–9), he knew he had to act upon that truth. There were two choices for Josiah: Either he would allow the idols to stay and just go along with it and reap the consequences of a godless society, or he would take action, do away with the idols, and incur the wrath of all those who worshipped them.

Josiah acted upon his newfound knowledge and upon truth. It came down to "Do I please the people? Or do I please the Lord God of Israel?" Josiah chose to please the Lord. His ultimate responsibility was to the Lord. The bottom line is not "What do people think?" but "What does God think?" Josiah made the decision to destroy the evil cults, including the temples, shrines, and altars that represent them. I am sure that his decision was not a very popular one with most of the people.

The Phases of Purging

The Purging of Judah and Jerusalem

Second Chronicles 34:3b–5, "In his twelfth year he began to purge Judah and Jerusalem of high places, Asherah poles, and idols." Under his direction, the altars of the Baalim were torn down; he cut to pieces the incense altars that were above them and smashed the Asherah poles, the idols, and the images. These he broke to pieces and scattered over the graves of those who had sacrificed to them. He burned the bones of the priests on their altars, and so he purged Judah and Jerusalem.

During his time of seeking the God of Abraham, Isaac, and Jacob, he developed a genuine hatred for sin, wickedness, and the worship of other gods. If it went against what the Law taught, he was adamantly against it. He had so given himself to the Lord that he would do anything to keep the Law and obey God.

So, the question was, "What was he to do about it?" The answer seems to have been clear to him. He must do away with all of those practices that would displease God. That included doing away with the very appearance of those evil practices; their shrines, altars, and temples. The worship of other gods was so prevalent and ingrained that it was the way of life for most of those in Judah and Jerusalem and permeated their culture and worship. Because it was so prevalent, it would take time to destroy and do away with them, even though every one of them was forbidden by God and the Law.

Scripture says that in the twelfth year, Josiah began to purge the land. This would take some time to accomplish. And he bravely led the way. Look at what he did:

1. They broke down the altars of the Baalim in his presence.

2. They hewed down the sun images on the high places.

3. They destroyed the Asherim and the graven images.

4. The molten images he broke into pieces.

5. He made dust from the molten images and sprinkled it on the graves of those who sacrificed to them.

6. He burnt the bones of the priests (of Baal) upon the altars on which they sacrificed.

To get a picture of the wickedness of the religions of the Canaanites, let's look at two of them, Baal and Molech.

Baal

Baal was their principal god; Ashtoreth, Baal's wife, their principal goddess. She was the personification of the reproductive principle in nature. Ishtar was her Babylonian name, and Astarte was her Greek and Roman name. Ashera was a sacred pole, cone of stone, or a tree trunk, representing the goddess. Temples of Baal and Ashtoreth were usually together. Priestesses were temple prostitutes. Sodomites were male temple prostitutes. The worship of Baal, Ashtoreth, and other Canaanite gods consisted in the most extravagant orgies; their temples were centers of vice (*Halley's Bible Handbook*, Religions of the Canaanites, page 166).

Their worship practice was for the priests of Baal and the priestesses of Ashteroth to engage in sexual intercourse during their ceremony, and the babies born of this religious practice were then offered in sacrifice to the gods of Baal and Ashteroth. So, in large measure, the land of Canaan had become sort of Sodom and Gomorrah on a national scale. Do we wonder why God commanded Israel to exterminate the Canaanites? Did a civilization of such abominable filth and brutality have any longer the right to exist? This is one example of the wrath of God against wickedness.

In an archaeological excavation at Gezer, Macalister, of the Palestine Exploration fund (1904–1909) found the ruins of a "High Place," which had been a temple in which they worshiped their god Baal and their goddess Ashtoreth. Under the debris, in this high place, they found great numbers of jars containing the remains of children who had been sacrificed to Baal. The whole area proved to be a cemetery for newborn babies (*Halley's Bible Handbook*, Religions of the Canaanites, page 166).

Molech

It usually is assumed that the cult of Molech involved sacrificing the children by throwing them into a raging fire. The expression "passed through the fire to Molech" (Leviticus 18:21; 2 Kings 23:10; Jeremiah 32:35) normally is so interpreted for these three reasons:

1. It is assumed that the same rite is mentioned in

2 Kings 16:3; 21:6; 23:6; Isaiah 30:33; Jeremiah 7:31; Deuteronomy 12:31.

2. This rite is abundantly verified among the Canaanites in both literary texts and artifactual evidence.

3. Whereas 2 Kings 23:10 informs us that Josiah defiled Topheth (incinerator) in the Valley of Ben Hinnom that no one might make his son or daughter pass through the fire to the "Molech." Jeremiah 7:31 says: "They have built the high place of Topheth in the Valley of Ben Hinnom to burn their sons and their daughters." The verbal connection between these two passages is so close that "to burn" seems to be equivalent to "pass through the fire" (*The Zondervan Pictorial Encyclopedia of the Bible*, by Merrill C. Tenney. Vol. 4, page 269).

Both 2 Kings 21:6 and 2 Chronicles 33:6 give the account of King Manasseh and his sin, which so provoked God to anger that He sent Judah away into captivity.

> *He sacrificed his children in the fire in the Valley of Ben Hinnom, practiced divination and witchcraft, sought omens, and consulted mediums and spiritists. He did much evil in the eyes of the Lord, arousing his anger.*
>
> **2 Chronicles 33:6**

So, it is no wonder that God's wrath was upon Judah, and He sent her away into the Babylonian captivity for seventy years. But for the fact that Josiah was, in contrast to Manasseh, so godly they would have been sent away sooner.

There isn't any difference in what the Canaanites, the Hittites, the Moabites, the Ammonites, the Edomites, the

Philistines, and the Amorites were doing than what we, in our western culture, are doing today. They offered their children in sacrifice on the altar to their gods in an effort to appease their gods, while we are offering our children in sacrifice on the altar of abortion to satisfy our gods of pleasure, sex, lust, selfishness, and convenience. We in America have killed over 55 million babies since Roe vs. Wade in 1973. I wonder how much longer God is going to allow this to continue before He pours out His wrath upon us. Pretty soon, the cup of iniquity will be full and running over. May God help us to turn from our evil ways and call upon Him in repentance and ask for forgiveness and mercy.

Josiah started his campaign against idolatry in Judah and Jerusalem. The more he found, the more there was. It seemed that there would be no end to it. But instead of getting weary in the task, he stayed focused and completed the work.

The Purging of the Temple

The king ordered Hilkiah the high priest, the priests next in rank and the doorkeepers to remove from the temple of the Lord all the articles made for Baal and Asherah and all the starry hosts. He burned them outside Jerusalem in the fields of the Kidron Valley and took the ashes to Bethel. He did away with the idolatrous priests appointed by the kings of Judah to burn incense on the high places of the towns of Judah and on those around Jerusalem— those who burned incense to Baal, to the sun and moon, to the constellations and to all the starry hosts. He took the Asherah pole from the temple of the Lord to the Kidron Valley outside Jerusalem and burned it there. He ground it to powder and scattered the dust over the graves of the common people. He also tore down the quarters of the male shrine prostitutes that were in the temple of the Lord, the quarters where women did weaving for Asherah. Josiah brought all the priests from the towns of Judah and desecrated the high places, from Geba to Beersheba, where the priests had burned incense. He broke down the shrines at the gates at the entrance to the Gate of Joshua, the city governor, which is on the left of the city gate. Although the priests of the high places did not serve at the altar of the Lord in Jerusalem, they ate unleavened bread with their fellow priests. He desecrated Topheth, which was in the Valley of Ben Hinnom, so no one could use it to sacrifice their son or daughter in the fire to Molek. He removed from the entrance to the temple of the Lord the horses that the kings of Judah had dedicated to the sun. They were in the court near the room of an official named Nathan-Melek. Josiah then burned the chariots dedicated to the sun. He pulled down the altars the kings of Judah had erected on the roof near the upper room of Ahaz, and the altars Manasseh had built in the two courts of the temple of the Lord. He removed them from there, smashed them to pieces and threw the rubble into the Kidron Valley. The king also desecrated the high places that were east of Jerusalem on the south of the Hill of Corruption—the ones Solomon king of Israel had built for Ashtoreth the vile goddess of the Sidonians, for Chemosh the vile god of Moab, and for Molek the detestable god of the people of Ammon. Josiah smashed the sacred stones and cut down the Asherah poles and covered the sites with human bones.

2 Kings 23:4–14

The fact that the temple of God was so polluted by heathen gods and goddesses must have been especially difficult for Josiah to stomach. And the unfortunate thing was that it was desecrated by former kings of Judah. They brought the altars and the shrines into the courtyard of the temple. What an abomination to God! Josiah systematically, purposely, and methodically dismantled each one and disgraced them and those who worshipped them. Look at this purging process:

1. He ordered all the articles made for Baal, Asherah, and the stars be removed from the temple.

2. He burned them outside Jerusalem in the Kidron Valley and took the ashes to Bethel.

3. He did away with the pagan priests who were appointed by the kings of Judah to burn incense on the high places.

4. He took the Asherah poles from the temple and burned them in the Kidron Valley.

5. He ground them to powder and scattered the ashes over the graves of the common people who worshipped them.

6. He tore down the quarters of the male prostitutes, which were in the temple.

7. He desecrated the high places from Geba to Beersheba where the priests had burned incense.

8. He broke down the shrines at the gate of the city governor.

9. He desecrated Topheth in the Valley of Ben Hinnom, so no one could use it to sacrifice his son or daughter in the fire to Molech.

10. He removed the sacred horses to the sun god from the entrance of the temple.

11. He then burned the chariots dedicated to the sun.

12. He pulled down the altars the kings of Judah had erected on the roofs of Ahaz.

13. He removed the altars Manasseh had built in the two courts of the temple; he smashed them to pieces and threw the rubble into the Kidron Valley.

14. He desecrated the high places that overlooked the city of Jerusalem, called the Hill of Corruption that King Solomon had built for the gods of his wives: Ashtoreth, the vile goddess of the Sidonians; Chemosh, the vile god of Moab; and Molech, the detestable god of the people of Ammon.

15. He smashed the sacred stones and cut down the Asherah poles and covered the sites with human bones.

To express his anger, disdain, and disgust for these gods, shrines, and altar, after smashing them to pieces, he threw them into the Kidron Valley, which was used as the local garbage dump. He also defiled them, burning the bones of the priests on the very altars on which they had burned incense to their gods. Josiah stayed with this project until the temple was back to its original state for the purpose of worship to God.

This activity of Josiah reminds me of the action of Jesus when He came into the temple and found them selling animals for sacrifices—all at unfair prices—and He overturned their tables, drove them out of the temple, and reminded them of the scripture in Isaiah, "'My house will be called a house of prayer,' but you are making it 'a den of robers'" (Matthew 21:13).

We must be careful how we use our churches today, making sure they are used for His purposes and His glory.

The Purging of Israel

In the towns of Manasseh, Ephraim and Simeon,
as far as Naphtali, and in the ruins around them,
he tore down the altars and the Asherah poles and
crushed the idols to powder and cut to pieces all
the incense altars throughout Israel. Then he went
back to Jerusalem.

2 Chronicles 34:6–7

During this time in Josiah's reign, the Assyrian kingdom was collapsing, and its military and political influence were waning. Josiah's influence was on the rise, and he began again to have control over a greater portion of Israel.

For those living in Israel who were serving God and wanted to return to the God of their fathers, this was a great opportunity for them, and they relished the opportunity to return to serving God. But that was not the feeling of the majority of the population. They were so ingrained in their heathen practices and worship that they would rather have been left alone.

Josiah, on the other hand, saw this as an opportunity to take his reforms to the Jewish people in the northern kingdom as well. So, he proceeded to travel north and continue his purging of the land from idolatry. And he did it with as much intensity and thoroughness as he had displayed in Judah and Jerusalem.

A 300-Year-Old Prophecy Fulfilled

Even the altar at Bethel, the high place made by
Jeroboam son of Nebat, who had caused Israel to
sin—even that altar and high place he demolished.
He burned the high place and ground it to powder,

and burned the Asherah pole also. Then Josiah looked around, and when he saw the tombs that were there on the hillside, he had the bones removed from them and burned on the altar to defile it, in accordance with the word of the Lord proclaimed by the man of God who foretold these things. The king asked, "What is that tombstone I see?" The people of the city said, "It marks the tomb of the man of God who came from Judah and pronounced against the altar of Bethel the very things you have done to it." "Leave it alone," he said. "Don't let anyone disturb his bones." So they spared his bones and those of the prophet who had come from Samaria. Just as he had done at Bethel, Josiah removed all the shrines at the high places that the kings of Israel had built in the towns of Samaria that had aroused the Lord's anger. Josiah slaughtered all the priests of those high places on the altars and burned human bones on them. Then he went back to Jerusalem.

2 Kings 23:15–20

In the process of cleansing the country, he came to the altars at Bethel. This is the altar that Jeroboam set up so the people would not go to Jerusalem to worship. Josiah demolished those altars and the high places as well where they worshiped. He ground them to powder and burned their Asherah pole. He then proceeded to take the bones of the priests who sacrificed at these altars and burned them on the altar to defile them. This was in accordance with the prophecy by the "man of God" who came from Judah over 300 years before and prophesied by name the man who would do this.

Let's look again at that story:

By the word of the Lord a man of God came from Judah to Bethel, as Jeroboam was standing by the altar to make an offering. By the word of the Lord he cried out against the altar: "Altar, altar! This is what the Lord says: 'A son named Josiah will be born to the house of David. On you he will sacrifice the priests of the high places who now make offerings here, and human bones will be burned on you.'" That same day the man of God gave a sign: "This is the sign the Lord has declared: The altar will be split apart and the ashes on it will be poured out."

1 Kings 13:1–3

The "man of God" arrives at Bethel while Jeroboam is there making an offering. The "man of God" proclaims what the Lord had given him to say. Jeroboam tried to apprehend the "man of God" and, pointing to him, demanded that they seize him. But God intervened, and Jeroboam's hand shriveled up. And at the same time, the altar split apart, and the ashes poured out, verifying the Word of the Lord.

When King Jeroboam heard what the man of God cried out against the altar at Bethel, he stretched out his hand from the altar and said, "Seize him!" But the hand he stretched out toward the man shriveled up, so that he could not pull it back. Also, the altar was split apart and its ashes poured out according to the sign given by the man of God by the word of the Lord. Then the king said to the man of God, "Intercede with the Lord your God and pray for me that my hand may be restored." So the man of God interceded with the Lord, and the king's hand was restored and became as it was before.

1 Kings 13:4–6

When Josiah came to the tomb of the "man of God" who made the prophecy, he inquired whose tomb it was. The men of the city explained to Josiah the story of the "man of God" and that he had foretold that very event that Josiah was bringing to pass. Josiah ordered that his tomb be kept intact and that his bones not be defiled.

Josiah then continued his mission, destroying and defiling the shrines, altars, and high places throughout Samaria. But there was one more act that he did before going back to Jerusalem. Josiah slaughtered all the priests of those high places on their altars and had the bones of the dead priests of Bethel exhumed from their graves and burned on their altars, which was viewed as an extreme act of desecration. Then he returned to Jerusalem. The zeal and intensity with which Josiah carried out the cleansing of the land was of divine origin and speaks of the total commitment he had to serve the Lord.

Josiah Return to Judah and Jerusalem

Upon completion of the cleansing of the land, he returned to Jerusalem. He must have had a feeling of satisfaction in knowing that the evil and wicked practices of the heathen who practiced these rituals were, for the time, discontinued.

The Silent War

There is another problem on which the Word of God is silent, that being the opposition to what Josiah was doing. The worship of idols had been going on for many generations, and those who worshiped them would likely have rebelled against any intrusion into their religious life. It is interesting that God's Word doesn't mention anything about this problem. I am sure that Josiah had some backlash against his reforms. The Word of God records only the positive accomplishments of Josiah and is silent about those who opposed him. The very fact that there must have been opposition brings him to another dilemma. With what was he going to replace their heathen practices with? That takes us to our next study.

Principles for Life

1. It's Not Always Popular with People to Obey God's Voice

To obey God is costly and messy. It will take time and commitment. I must know that it is of God, then proceed with confidence.

2. Some of Your Friends May Oppose What You Are Doing

There will always be those who don't want to get involved. They don't want to put forth the effort or pay the price.

3. The Word of God Must Be Obeyed

We must live in obedience to His Word. Nothing else matters.

4. God Will Give You Strength to Carry Out His Word

When doing His will, God prepares, directs, gives direction and strength to carry it out.

5. Obeying God's Voice Brings a Personal Peace

Because His approval is more important than human approval, His peace sustains us.

6. There Will Be Those Who Will Follow Your Leadership

There will be those who are eager to follow you as you follow Christ.

7. When You Hear from God, Don't Listen to Another Voice

Not everyone will also have heard from the Lord and may try to talk you out of it.

8. You Will Not Grow without Purging Your Life of Idols

An idol is anything that takes the place of God in your life.

9. Purging Your Life Puts You in a Position to Receive from God

When you empty yourself of the things of the world, He will fill you up with Himself and new insight about who He is.

10. Discerning God's Voice Is a Matter of Life and Death

To put to death and root out the things that are not of God means death to the world, but you will rise with new life and a newfound reason for being.

11. "As for me and my household, we will serve the Lord" (Joshua 24:15b).

CHAPTER SIX:

Restoration and Discovery

In the eighteenth year of his reign, King Josiah sent the secretary, Shaphan son of Azaliah, the son of Meshullam, to the temple of the Lord. He said, "Go up to Hilkiah the high priest and have him get ready the money that has been brought into the temple of the Lord, which the doorkeepers have collected from the people. Have them entrust it to the men appointed to supervise the work on the temple. And have these men pay the workers who repair the temple of the Lord—the carpenters, the builders and the masons. Also have them purchase timber and dressed stone to repair the temple. But they need not account for the money entrusted to them, because they are acting faithfully.

2 Kings 22:3–7

*In the eighteenth year of Josiah's reign, to purify
the land and the temple, he sent Shaphan the son
of Azaliah and Maaseiah the ruler of the city,
with Joah son of Joahaz, the recorder, to repair
the temple of the Lord his God. They went to
Hilkiah the high priest and gave him the money
that had been brought into the temple of God,
which the Levites who were the gatekeepers had
collected from the people of Manasseh, Ephraim
and the entire remnant of Israel and from all the
people of Judah and Benjamin and the inhabitants
of Jerusalem. Then they entrusted it to the men
appointed to supervise the work on the Lord's
temple. These men paid the workers who repaired
and restored the temple. They also gave money to
the carpenters and builders to purchase dressed
stone, and timber for the joists and beams for the
buildings that the kings of Judah had allowed to
fall into ruin. The workers labored faithfully. Over
them to direct them were Jahath and Obadiah,
Levites descended from Merari, and Zechariah
and Meshullam, descended from Kohath. The
Levites—all who were skilled in playing musical
instruments—had charge of the laborers and
supervised all the workers from job to job. Some
of the Levites were secretaries, scribes and
gatekeepers.*

2 Chronicles 34:8–13

A Time of Transition

Where to Go from Here

Josiah is now in his eighteenth year as king, and he is
twenty-six years old. He was at that time in his life when
most young men want to experience life, sow their wild oats,

do their own thing, and "make their mark" in the world. But instead of being known as a party person, he is known as a worshiper of God.

Josiah had come through his early life of influence, a time when others determined to a great degree what they would do and who they wanted to be. But Josiah went through his own personal search to discover who God was for himself. Following that, he went on a campaign to cleanse the land, in which he tore down the altars, shrines, and temples to heathen gods, which were forbidden by God for Israel. Now it was time for him to give himself to the God he heard about, searched for, and for which he campaigned.

By this time in Josiah's reign, there were three that were influential in his life:

1. The prophet Zephaniah, his relative and contemporary.

2. The prophet Jeremiah, who began his ministry during the thirteenth year of Josiah's reign (Jeremiah 1:1). (Jeremiah's prophetic ministry had been going on for five years when Josiah began to repair the temple.)

3. The high priest Hilkiah, with whom Josiah had a close personal relationship.

All these people no doubt had an impact on Josiah's life by this time, and their impact greatly affected the decisions that Josiah was making.

For six years, Josiah gave himself to purging not only the country of Judah but also the northern country of Israel. But now, the campaigns were over. For the past six years, he had been on a mission, a cause, to cleanse the land, and he was the talk of the land, both in Judah and Israel. Many were for him and were glad to see the reforms that were being done and rejoiced with what they were seeing. On the other hand, most of the people were so ingrained into heathen worship. They saw his work as meddling in their lives and affairs. (This is evidenced by the fact that when Josiah died, the people immediately went right back into idol worship.) Josiah had likely polarized the country. They were either solidly for him, or they were adamantly against him. There were those who spoke of him with great reverence and respect, and then there were those who spoke of him with disdain and hatred.

There is a certain intoxication associated with "causes." People can get caught up in the "cause" of serving God and miss the relationship with Him. There is the danger of always having a "cause" for which to give oneself, rather than giving yourself to God and letting Him use you in whatever cause He chooses. Some never come to a real giving of themselves to the God they say they serve. Rather it's the "cause" they serve. May God help us not to serve "causes" so we can give ourselves to serving Him.

When serving the Lord is more important than your relationship with Him, then you are only serving a "cause" and not the Lord. If your relationship with Christ depends on whether you are working with Sunday school, the youth, the outreach program, choir, drama, benevolence, or any other program in the church, then check your motives. You may just be serving a cause. Josiah had been through all of that, and now he wanted to give himself to his God and build a relationship with Him.

Are You a Server or a Worshiper?

There are those who always serve the Lord and never worship the Lord. They are always busy doing something for the Lord but never spending time communing with Him and basking in His presence. Mary and Martha are good examples of the difference between a server and a worshipper.

> *As Jesus and his disciples were on their way, he came to a village where a woman named Martha opened her home to him. She had a sister called Mary, who sat at the Lord's feet listening to what he said. But Martha was distracted by all the preparations that had to be made. She came to him and asked, "Lord, don't you care that my sister has left me to do the work by myself? Tell her to help me!" "Martha, Martha," the Lord answered, "you are worried and upset about many things, but few things are needed—or indeed only one. Mary has chosen what is better, and it will not be taken away from her."*

Luke 10:38–42

May the Lord help us to become like Mary; just enjoy His presence.

Restoring the House of God

The Temple Restored to Its Rightful Prominence

> *In the eighteenth year of Josiah's reign, to purify the land and the temple, he sent Shaphan ...and Maaseiah the ruler of the city, with Joah ...the recorder, to repair the temple of the Lord his God.*

2 Chronicles 34:8

During the years of Josiah's father and grandfather, the temple had gone into disrepair from sheer neglect. Because it was placed in a position of unimportance in Judah's life and worship, there was no reason to maintain it. With Josiah's reforms in place, that was soon to change. The temple was again to be the focal point of Judah's worship, social culture, and way of life.

Josiah placed Shaphan, the Secretary of State, Maaseiah, the mayor of the city, and Joah, the recorder (or historian) as project managers over the repair of the temple. They, in turn, went to Hilkiah, the high priest, with the money that had been collected for that purpose with instructions to proceed with the repairs. The money had been collected from both Judah and Israel. These men hired the carpenters and stonemasons and purchased the stones, joists, beams, and timbers to be used in the repair work. They also appointed four Levites, Jahath, Obadiah, Zechariah, and Meshullam as supervisors over the laborers and workers. The Bible says, "The workers labored faithfully" (2 Chronicles 34:12), and "they need not give an account for the money entrusted to them, because they were acting faithfully" (2 Kings 22:7).

Make God's House a Priority in Your Life

Once again, Josiah made the worship of God and the temple experience important to the lives of the people. We, too, must keep God's house and our worship there a high priority in our lives. It is very important to maintain our relationship with our brothers and sisters in Christ and for our growth in the Lord. This is what God's Word says to us about this. "Not giving up meeting together, as some are in the habit of doing, but encouraging one another—and all the more as you see the Day approaching" (Hebrews 10:25).

We need one another. We need others to pray for us and we for them; we need to hear how God is working in their lives, and they need to hear what He is doing in ours. We need to hear the Word of God taught and preached to receive help for our daily lives. There are a lot of distractions that keep us from God's house, but we must not let them rob us of what God wants to do for us as we worship together in His house. When we have an intimate, dynamic, personal relationship with the Lord, we also find that attending the house of the Lord is not a burden but rather a pleasurable, enjoyable, and growing experience.

The Proper Use of God's Money

> *They went to Hilkiah the high priest and gave him the money that had been brought into the temple of God, which the Levites who were the gatekeepers had collected from the people of Manasseh, Ephraim and the entire remnant of Israel and from all the people of Judah and Benjamin and the inhabitants of Jerusalem.*
>
> **2 Chronicles 34:9**

The Word of God gives specific instructions about our finances and how much of it belongs to Him. The money collected for the use and upkeep of God's house should be used for that purpose. The Bible says in Malachi 3:8–12:

> *"Will a mere mortal rob God? Yet you rob me. But you ask, 'How do we rob you?' In tithes and offerings. You are under a curse—your whole nation—because you are robbing me. Bring the whole tithe into the storehouse, that there may be food in my house. Test me in this," says the Lord Almighty, "and see if I will not throw open the floodgates of heaven and pour out so much blessing that you will not have room enough to store it. I will prevent pests from devouring your crops, and the vines in your fields will not drop their fruit before it is ripe," says the Lord Almighty. "Then all the nations will call you blessed, for yours will be a delightful land," says the Lord Almighty.*

In short, what God is saying is that if you give your tithes (one-tenth) to Him, He will make the ninety percent that you keep for your personal use go farther than if you would keep the whole one hundred percent for yourself.

The tithe belongs to the Lord! So, give it to Him. If you are struggling with your finances and you are not tithing, it probably won't get better until you do. God is faithful! Those who are faithful in tithing will find God faithful to them. When we realize that all we have is the Lord's anyway, it is not hard to give it to Him.

While pastoring in Ephrata, Washington, I had an occasion to witness God's provision because of faithfulness in tithing. Our neighbor, Al, who was also a member of our church, was having trouble with his finances. He came to see me and explained why it was impossible for him to tithe. It wasn't because he was irresponsible with his finances; he simply did not have enough money to go around. I challenged him to start tithing and see what God would do to provide for him. I assured him that God's promise was if he would tithe, God would make his money go around. I encouraged him to do this for three months straight. He said he would try it. One month later, he came to see me and complained that now it was even worse than before but confessed he had only been giving 5 percent instead of 10 percent. Again, I told him that God's Word is true, and he had to give the 10 percent for this to work. Then I added, "If after three months if you don't see that God's Word is true, then you bring me your bills, and I will pay them." Before the three months were over, he came over again, and this time, he was rejoicing, and he was shouting, "It works! It works!" God had worked in such a way in his finances that he was able not only to pay his tithes but give to missions as well. From that time on, nothing stopped him from tithing. He saw how tithing worked on his behalf.

I also saw this principle work on the corporate level. I believe that not only does God provide for those who tithe personally, but the principle also applies corporately as well. What we give to missions should be an amount equal to at least a tithe of our church income. (Our church regularly gave between 15 percent and 20 percent to missions.) When we started to build our new sanctuary for the church, they (the membership) decided to tithe from our building fund. We gave 10 percent to other churches or missions programs that were building because the money was donated to our church for construction. We also decided to build for cash. In the process of over five years, we gave away over $27,000, and in the end, we realized that the Lord returned to us roughly five dollars for every dollar we gave away. *You cannot outgive God!*

The text further states that they need not account for the money entrusted to them because they acted faithfully (2 Kings 22:7).

This does not necessarily mean that they didn't keep a record of what they spent and what it was used for. What it does mean is that those who were in charge were men of such honor and integrity that their fidelity was not called into question. There was no misappropriation of the funds given to them for the repair of the temple.

It is important that accurate records be kept and that they be made available to all who want to see them. It is a shame when those in charge of God's money misuse it or steal it for their own use. God has promised that He will supply all our needs, so why do I need to steal from Him. I heard one pastor say, tongue in cheek, "If you have friends who do not tithe when they come over to your house, keep an eye on them because if they steal from God, they will steal from anybody."

Honoring Other Members of the Body of Christ

Then they entrusted it to the men appointed to supervise the work on the Lord's temple. These men paid the workers who repaired and restored the temple. They also gave money to the carpenters and builders to purchase dressed stone, and timbers for joists and beams for the buildings that the kings of Judah had allowed to fall into ruin (2 Kings 22:10–11).

When we recognize the fact that God is able to use others in the body of Christ, we can truly rejoice with them and thank God for them. How freeing it is to allow God to use others in doing the work of the ministry. Everyone has their place within the body of Christ. God can, will, and does use others for His glory as He sees fit.

In 1 Corinthians 12:12–27, Paul explains how the body of Christ is to function together:

> *Just as a body, though one, has many parts, but all its many parts form one body, so it is with Christ. For we were all baptized by one Spirit so as to form one body—whether Jews or Greeks, slave or free—and we were all given the one Spirit to drink. Even so the body is not made up of one part but of many. Now if the foot should say, "Because I am not a hand, I do not belong to the body," it would not for that reason stop being part of the body. And if the ear should say, "Because I am not an eye, I do not belong to the body," it would not for that reason stop being part of the body. If the whole body were an eye, where would the sense of hearing be? If the whole body were an ear, where would the sense of smell be? But in fact God has placed the parts in the body, every one of them, just as he wanted them to be. If they were all one*

134

*part, where would the body be? As it is, there are
many parts, but one body. The eye cannot say to the
hand, "I don't need you!" And the head cannot say
to the feet, "I don't need you!" On the contrary,
those parts of the body that seem to be weaker
are indispensable, and the parts that we think are
less honorable we treat with special honor. And
the parts that are unpresentable are treated with
special modesty, while our presentable parts need
no special treatment. But God has put the body
together, giving greater honor to the parts that
lacked it, so that there should be no division in the
body, but that its parts should have equal concern
for each other. If one part suffers, every part suffers
with it; if one part is honored, every part rejoices
with it. Now you are the body of Christ, and each
one of you is a part of it.*

All the Work Was Done in Harmony

*The workers labored faithfully. Over them to direct
them were Jahath and Obadiah, Levites descended
from Merari, and Zechariah and Meshullam,
descended from Kohath. The Levites—all who
were skilled in playing musical instruments—
had charge of the laborers and supervised all the
workers from job to job. Some of the Levites were
secretaries, scribes and gatekeepers.*

2 Chronicles 34:12–13

Not only did the Levites engage in the worship and offering
the sacrifices to the Lord, but they were also the caretakers of
the temple and the sacred articles of the temple. So, it was
their responsibility to care for, clean, and repair the temple,
the instruments, and the furnishings. So, using them was in

keeping with the proper procedure and care of the temple.

Paul says in Ephesians 5:21, "Submit to one another out of reverence for Christ." Scripture further states,

> *Have confidence in your leaders and submit to their authority, because they keep watch over you as those who must give an account. Do this so that their work will be a joy, not a burden, for that would be of no benefit to you.*

Hebrews 13:17

There will always be someone to whom we must give an account. God knew that we could not handle unchallenged authority. So, in His wisdom, He made it possible for us to be accountable to others. When everyone works together, everything is in harmony.

The story of the nose, the eyes, and the glasses probably illustrates this better than anything else.

One day the nose said to the eyes, "I am tired of carrying your glasses for you. You are going to have to find some other means by which to hold them." The eyes pleaded with the nose and assured him that there was no one else who could do the job as he did. But to no avail. The nose gave notice that on Friday at 3 p.m., he would no longer hold or carry the eyes' glasses. Though the eyes pleaded, the nose would not relent, and at 3 p.m. on Friday, the glasses came off.

Later on, that evening, after the sunset, the legs were carrying the body down the street on the way home for the night. But because it was getting dark, and the eyes no longer had the assistance of the nose to hold his glasses, he didn't see the curb and tripped. He went sprawling, going end over end, coming to rest on the nose. When he was finally able to collect himself and got to his feet, the nose said to the eyes, "I think we had better get the glasses."

When we get our priorities squared away with the Lord and in their proper place, it is amazing how harmoniously things work together. But when I am still serving a "cause," things are chaotic, and there is disunity and contention. Why? Because whatever *your* "cause" is, it is not as important as the "cause" that *I* am doing. When we get ourselves in proper alignment in the service of God, it is amazing how much I now appreciate my fellow workers. We then can accept and appreciate others' ministry within the body of Christ.

The King's Orders Were Carried Out

> *Then Shaphan the secretary went to the King and reported to him: "Your officials have paid out the money that was in the temple of the Lord and have entrusted it to the workers and supervisors at the temple."*

2 Kings 22:9

"The workers labored faithfully. Over them to direct them were Jahath and Obadiah, Levites descended from Merari, and Zechariah and Meshullam, descended from Kohath" (2 Chronicles 34:12).

When the work on the temple was completed, Shaphan, the secretary, reported back to the king that his orders had been carried out. The temple had been cleansed and repaired, and that it was now ready for its intended purpose and use—the worship of the Lord. There is a twofold message here:

1. Those placed in charge of the repair were held accountable and reported back to the king that they had done everything he had requested.

2. Those who did the actual work did it faithfully.

There is a sense of accomplishment when a job is completed. There is also a sense of satisfaction in knowing that not only that the job was completed, but that it was done well. Those who had done the work were skilled craftsmen and did the best job they could do. There was a double sense of urgency for this job because it was not only for the king but was also for the house of God. There was a chain of command involved in the work. First, there was the king who gave the order; then the officials who were responsible for carrying it out; then the high priest who was responsible for the temple; then, the Levites who were the supervisors of the workers; and then the workers themselves. They all faithfully carried out their parts of the restoration. And in each step, there was accountability to those who were just above them.

When giving out responsibility, there must also be accountability. When there is no accountability, there is chaos. We all work better when we must give an account of what we have done. That principle plays out throughout our entire lives and will conclude when we stand before God and give an account of our lives before Him.

Principles for Life

1. Everyone Must Choose to Commit to Christ

You will come to the time when you must make a choice about Christ being Lord of your life. It is a turning point as to which way you will go.

2. God's House Must Have a Prominent Place in Your Life

Along with serving the Lord is the coming together for worship with others of the family of God. Don't let other things distract you from God's house.

3. Make Him Lord of Your Finances

The tithe belongs to the Lord. When He is Lord of your money, He will supply all your needs.

4. There Are No Lone-Rangers in the Work of the Kingdom

God has strategically placed in the body of Christ others who He has placed His hands onto accomplish His work and bring it to completion.

5. When Everything Is in Order There Is Peace and Harmony

When everyone functions where God has placed them within the body of Christ, there is peace and harmony. People love one another, God is glorified, and the church is a powerful testimony to the community of true Christianity.

6. The Work of the Kingdom Is Accomplished

CHAPTER SEVEN:
New Revelation

While they were bringing out the money that had been taken into the temple of the Lord, Hilkiah the priest found the Book of the Law of the Lord that had been given through Moses. Hilkiah said to Shaphan the secretary, "I have found the Book of the Law in the temple of the Lord." He gave it to Shaphan. Then Shaphan took the book to the king and reported to him: "Your officials are doing everything that has been committed to them. They have paid out the money that was in the temple of the Lord and have entrusted it to the supervisors and workers." Then Shaphan the secretary informed the king, "Hilkiah the priest has given me a book." And Shaphan read from it in the presence of the king.

2 Chronicles 34:14–18

Hilkiah the high priest said to Shaphan the secretary, "I have found the Book of the Law in the temple of the Lord." He gave it to Shaphan, who read it. Then Shaphan the secretary went to the king and reported to him: "Your officials have paid out the money that was in the temple of the Lord and have entrusted it to the workers and supervisors at the temple." Then Shaphan the secretary informed the king, "Hilkiah the priest has given me a book." And Shaphan read from it in the presence of the king.

2 Kings 22:8–10

"Neither before nor after Josiah was there a king like him who turned to the Lord ...with all his heart and with all his soul and with all his strength" (2 Kings 23:25).

The Book of the Law Found

God Prepares Josiah for His Law

Josiah was one of only a few kings who gave himself completely to serving God with all his heart. That alone is perhaps the most important thing that stands out about his life and character above everything else. What an incredible testimony about a man's life, "He gave himself totally to serve the Lord with all his heart, soul, and strength."

He purged the land of Judah and Jerusalem, the temple, and the land of Israel of all the heathen idols, which were an abomination in God's sight. The next step was to repair and restore the temple to its proper use for worship. Note, the restoration of the temple came after the cleansing of the land. The casting out of idols must always precede the building or repairing of the temple of God so worship can proceed according to God's divine order. God said,

> *You shall have no other gods before me. You shall*
> *not make for yourself an image in any form of*
> *anything in heaven above or on the earth beneath*
> *or in the waters below. You shall not bow down to*
> *them or worship them.*

Deuteronomy 5:7–9

One of the things that I have observed is that many people want to just add the serving of God to the bag of "gods" they already serve. I guess they figure that they have everything covered this way. But God will not have it that way. It must be Him and Him alone, or it is idolatry. The interesting thing about this commandment is that it is the one that comes with a blessing or cursing.

> *You shall not bow down to them or worship them;*
> *for I, the Lord your God, am a jealous God,*
> *punishing the children for the sin of the parents to*
> *the third and fourth generation of those who hate*
> *me, but showing love to a thousand generations of*
> *those who love me and keep my commandments.*

Deuteronomy 5:9–10

This is the reason that when going into an area where the gospel has not been preached, it is important that the people who convert to Christianity renounce all other gods. This is the one area where there can be no compromise. There must be *no other gods*!

The commitment to serving God that Josiah displayed had not existed like this since the days of King David and King Solomon. Just as he had given himself to destroying the idols from the land, so now he gave himself to with the same intensity to serving God and preparing the temple so this could happen. Wherever there are hearts searching after God,

He will respond and reveal Himself to them. Josiah was about to experience that. Jesus said in the sermon on the mount:

> *Ask and it will be given to you; seek and you will find; knock and the door will be opened to you. For everyone who asks receives; the one who seeks finds; and the one who knocks, the door will be opened.*

Matthew 7:7–8

Two Questions about the Finding of the Law

What was it they found?

Most scholars think that the portion of the Law of Moses that was found in the temple was the book of Deuteronomy. Some think that they may have also found the book of Exodus.

Where did they find it?

The book may have been hidden by the priests during the days of Manasseh's terrible persecution when his emphasis was on the worship of foreign gods. Honorable priests may have hidden it in fear of its total destruction by a godless king. Some theorize that there were those who were out to destroy it, and, therefore, it was deliberately hidden for preservation, perhaps in the temple foundation where it would be safe. This would explain why it was found while the temple was being repaired. Others think that the Law had so grown in disfavor that it got neglected and was just set aside, or, maybe put into a corner where it was just ignored, and other things were placed on top of it, so, for all practical purposes, it was hidden. Some speculate that it was placed in the treasure chest where the money was placed for the upkeep of the temple. The authors of the *Pulpit Commentary* suggest that it may have been kept in the ark of the covenant and was found there (vol. 4, page 423). In any event, the text says, "Hilkiah the high priest said to Shaphan the secretary, 'I have found the Book of the Law in the temple of the Lord'" (2 Kings 22:8).

The Preservation of God's Word

The fact that the book of the Law was *found* infers that it had been lost. There is no mention of how long it had been lost. But the fact that it had been so carelessly kept is indicative of the indifference and disregard for its importance by the priests and kings who were its appointed guardians. In this story, we see an instance of the indestructibility of God's Word. His Word is imperishable. There is a divine hand guarding this very precious writing called the Book of the Law. The permanence of the written Word, the providence that watched over it, the romantic history of its preservation through ages of neglect, and the timely rediscovery of the Book of the Law speaks to the reliability and importance to its author. After all, it is called "God's Word."

The finding of the Book of the Law of Moses was by no means "just coincidental." All believe that it was preserved by the Lord for just such a time as this. Whether it was lost by carelessness or hidden by design, God was in control of its safety and preservation. God has always preserved His Word and will through all generations until His return. This was confirmed when Jesus said, "Heaven and earth will pass away, but my words will never pass away" (Matthew 24:35).

Incredible Non-Coincidence

The late Dr. Bill Bright, founder and chairman of Campus Crusade for Christ, tells a story that makes this point about God's preservation of His Word and His control over

145

situations. There are no accidents with God.

In the 1930s, Stalin ordered a purge of all Bibles and all believers in the former Soviet Union. Millions of Bibles were confiscated, and multitudes of believers were sent to Gulags (prison camps), where most died for being "enemies of the state." In Stavropol, Russia, this order was carried out with a vengeance.

Recently, the CoMission Ministry, sponsored by Campus Crusade for Christ, sent a team to Stavropol, Russia. The city's history was not known to the team at the time. But when the team was having difficulties getting Bibles shipped from Moscow, someone mentioned the existence of a warehouse outside of town where these confiscated Bibles had been stored ever since Stalin's days.

After much prayer by the team, one member finally got up the courage to go to the warehouse and ask the officials if the Bibles were still there. Sure enough, they were. Then the CoMission asked if the Bibles could be removed and distributed again to the people of Stavropol. The answer was "Yes!"

The next day the CoMission team returned with a truck and several Russian people to help load the Bibles. One helper was a young man, who was a skeptical, hostile, and agnostic collegian who had come only for the day's wages.

As they were loading the Bibles, one team member noticed that the young man had disappeared. Eventually, they found him in a corner of the warehouse weeping.

He had slipped away, hoping to quietly take a Bible. What he found shook him to the core. The inside page of the Bible he picked up had the handwritten signature of his own grandmother! It had been her Bible! Out of the many thousands of Bibles still left in that warehouse, he stole the one belonging to his grandmother—a woman persecuted for her faith all her life.

No wonder he was weeping; God had just dramatically revealed Himself to this young man. His grandmother had no doubt prayed for him and for her city. Her prayers had followed him, and now this young man's life has been transformed by the very Bible that his grandmother cherished and found so dear.

"Oh, the depth of the riches both of the wisdom and knowledge of God! How unsearchable his judgments, and his paths beyond tracing out!" (Romans 11:33).

While Doing the Work, We Found the Book of the Law

"Hilkiah the high priest said unto Shaphan the secretary, 'I have found the Book of the Law in the temple of the Lord'" (2 Kings 22:8).

Hilkiah the priest found the Book of the Law of the Lord that had been given through Moses. Hilkiah said to Shaphan the secretary, "I have found the Book of the Law in the temple of the Lord."

2 Chronicles 34:14–15

One of the interesting things about this story is that they were not looking for the Book of the Law, they were going about the work of repairing the temple when they happened upon it, but it was by divine providence. They found it right where it was supposed to be, in the temple. It is interesting that when we begin searching for the Lord, we find Him right where we have left Him.

How tragic it is when the Word of God is lost in the temple. God's Word should be the central focus of His house. It must be the read, preached, and taught from our pulpits.

When churches proclaim another gospel other than the pure Word of God in His house, we are going down the road to serving idols. May God give us ministers who will boldly proclaim His Word.

It is noteworthy that it was while they were doing the necessary mundane things in the repair and renovation of the temple that they found the Word of the Lord. Sometimes we have in mind that we must do something spectacular so God will use us. It is while we are faithful in the little things that the Lord will put His hand upon us for use in greater ways. Don't worry about doing spectacular things for God; rather, remain faithful where He has placed you. If your heart is hungry for God, keep on doing the things you have been doing where He has placed you, and He will reveal the next step He has for your life. When we prove ourselves faithful in the little things, then He can entrust us with greater responsibilities. Peter addresses this in his epistle: "Humble yourselves, therefore, under God's mighty hand, that he may lift you up in due time" (1 Peter 5:6).

In 2 Kings 5, we read the story of a faithful little servant girl in the household of Naaman, as a servant to his wife. She told her mistress about Elisha: "If only my master would see the prophet who is in Samaria! He would cure him of his leprosy" (2 Kings 5:3). This is a little girl who was taken captive by a hostile invading army but remained true to her God. As a result, Naaman was cured of leprosy. But it started with one little girl who was faithful to God as a servant.

We see this principle played out time after time in Scripture. Remember, it was while David was tending his family's sheep that he was called in from the field and anointed by Samuel to be king over Israel. It was while Moses was tending his father-in-law's sheep out in the desert that God appeared to him in a burning bush and commissioned him to go back to

Egypt and lead the children of Israel out of slavery. It was while Elisha was plowing his field that Elijah threw his cloak around him and commissioned him to be his successor as the next prophet in Israel. It was while Andrew, Peter, James, and John were fishing that Jesus called them to come, follow Him, and be His disciples. "'Come follow me,' Jesus said, 'and I will send you out to fish for people'" (Mark 1:17).

When in the service of the Lord, we don't have to do something big or impressive to get His attention, for He knows where we are and what we are doing, and He will come, call us, prepare us, and commission us to follow Him. Let Him exalt you in His time.

The Sharing of the Book of the Law

The Book of the Law Shared with the King

Then Shaphan took the book to the king and reported to him: "Your officials are doing everything that has been committed to them. They have paid out the money that was in the temple of the Lord and have entrusted it to the supervisors and workers." Then Shaphan the secretary informed the king, "Hilkiah the priest has given me a book." And Shaphan read from it in the presence of the king.

2 Chronicles 34:16–18

"Then Shaphan the secretary informed the king, 'Hilkiah the priest has given me a book.' And Shaphan read from it in the presence of the king" (2 Kings 22:10).

When Hilkiah, the high priest, found the Book of the Law, he did not keep it to himself, but he shared it with King Josiah. Hilkiah could have reasoned that as the high priest, it was his responsibility to keep and take care of the Book of the Law, but he immediately shared it with Shaphan, who, in turn, read it and shared it with the king.

The revelation of God's Word to us is something to be shared. This is especially true of those in authority. They need to know what God's Word is saying to them. There is no other written document that is as important as God's Word.

This was an automatic thing with Hilkiah and Shaphan. There was no hesitancy on their part about sharing what they had found with the king. The Book of the Law was found and given to Hilkiah, who in turn gave it to Shaphan, who in turn took it to the king and shared it with him.

The Importance of Sharing God's Word

It is imperative that we, too, share what we know with others. That is what the "great commission" is all about. In fact, one of Jesus' last acts with His disciples was to give them this directive. In Matthew's Gospel, He gives it.

> *All authority in heaven and on earth has been given to me. Therefore, go and make disciples of all nations, baptizing them in the name of the Father and of the Son and of the Holy Spirit, and teaching them to obey everything I have commanded you. And surely I am with you always, unto the end of the age.*

Matthew 28:18–20

And it is repeated in Mark's Gospel, "Go into all the world and preach the gospel to all creation" (Mark 16:15).

Not only did He tell us to go and proclaim this good news, but He also told us that He would give us a helper so we could do it. In John's Gospel, Jesus said,

*When the Advocate comes, whom I will send to you
from the Father—the Spirit of truth who goes out
from the Father—He will testify about me. And you
also must testify, for you have been with me from
the beginning.*

John 15:26–27

"You will receive power when the Holy Spirit comes on you; and you shall be my witnesses in Jerusalem, and in all Judea and Samaria, and to the ends of the earth" (Acts 1:8).

We have not only been commissioned to proclaim Him as Savior, but He has given us the Holy Spirit to empower us to share it. Does that mean I must be a preacher or missionary? No, but it does mean that I must share it where I am and with those with whom I come in contact. What we share truly is "the good news," for it is the only way for people to know God.

The "good news" is for everybody. The educated, the uneducated, royalty, heads of state, rich, poor, CEOs, white-collar, blue-collar, old, young, all races, every social class, men, women, all must hear God's Word. And it is our privilege and opportunity to share this "good news."

Begin Sharing God's Word at Home

Parents have the greatest opportunity to instruct and lead their children to know Christ as their Savior. Parents must so train their children in the Word of God that they will, without hesitation, make the will of God the greatest ambition of their lives. It must start at home and goes out from there.

Fanny Crosby, the great blind hymn writer, testifies to the start she received from her grandmother. Fanny's trustful spirit found its anchor in the Word of God because of this essential role her grandmother played. When Fanny was a little child, that good woman would take the little girl on her knee and read long passages of Scripture aloud. "It was Grandma who brought the Bible to me and me to the Bible," she remarked years later. She learned by heart several Old Testament books and most of the New Testament. Down through the years, God spoke to her, as friend to friend, through those Scriptures.

The Revelation of God to Mankind

God Reveals Himself to Josiah

God had revealed Himself before to mankind, but it was a new revelation of God to Josiah personally. What God had revealed to others previously, He was now personalizing for Josiah. Josiah had given himself to seeking God, and once he was convinced of the truth of God, he began to do away with those things that would interfere with that relationship. Josiah did away with the old ways that were dishonoring to the Lord and the wicked evil practices that offended Him. After cleansing the land, he proceeded to clear out the temple and restore it to the sole purpose of the worship of God alone.

In the process, they found the "Book of the Law of Moses." Within that book was a new revelation to Josiah about God and the demands that go along with that relationship with Him. With every relationship, there are certain demands that go along with it. There cannot be a passive relationship—there must be involvement. If there is no involvement, then there is only an acquaintance, not a relationship. In relationships, there are certain things that must be done and certain things that cannot be done. In our relationship with God, there are consequences if we do things we shouldn't or if we don't do things we should. This relationship with God is a covenant relationship, and in a covenant relationship, there are things binding for both parties. God's part of the covenant is to fulfill what He has promised to and for us. Our part is to live up to and fulfill our part of it. Josiah was about to find out that they had not kept their part of the covenant relationship and that there were dire consequences for breaking the covenant. They were about to incur God's wrath for breaking it. In Josiah's case, it is apparent that he was unaware of the imminent danger he was about to face (we will discuss this further in the next chapter).

God Wants to Reveal Himself to Us

When we are hungering and thirsting for the knowledge of God, He will respond to our searching hearts and reveal Himself to us. God wants each of us to know Him in an intimate way. Just as you have a relationship with your parents that is unique only to you, so too we can have a relationship with God that is very personal and intimate.

God's purpose for the creation of humankind was for a personal, intimate relationship with us. But He also created us with free will. It is His desire that we serve Him by choice, not as a programmed robot. Jesus came to earth to reveal the Father to us. When Philip asked Jesus, "Show us the Father," Jesus responded, "If you have seen me, you have seen the Father" (John 14:7–10). God's purpose in sending Jesus was two-fold:

1. To reveal to us who He is—that we might know Him (have a relationship with Him).

2. To provide salvation for us so we might have an eternal relationship with Him.

Paul said, "I want to know Christ" (Philippians 3:10). When we get to the place where we want nothing else than to know Him, when it is more important to us than our daily food, our rest, our job, our very life itself, then we can be confident He will reveal Himself to us. Oh God, give us this kind of hunger for You!

A word of warning:

The things God will reveal to us about Himself are in no way to go beyond what has been revealed through His Word. Paul warns us,

> *If we or an angel from heaven should preach to you a gospel other than the one we preached to you, let them be under God's curse! As we have already said, so now I say again: If anybody is preaching to you a gospel other than what you accepted, let them be under God's curse!*

Galatians 1:8–9

Any further revelation of God to us will be in keeping with what has already been revealed in Scripture.

We Are Commanded to Seek the Lord

God's Word instructs us to give ourselves to seek Him. Listen to His Word:

1. If from there you seek the Lord your God, you will find him if you seek him with all your heart and with all your soul (Deuteronomy 4:29).

2. David's instruction to his son Solomon when he became king of Israel:

> *You, my son Solomon, acknowledge the God of your father, and serve him with wholehearted devotion and with a willing mind, for the Lord searches every heart and understands every desire*

and every thought. If you seek him, he will be found by you; but if you forsake him, he will reject you forever.

1 Chronicles 28:9

"You will seek me and find me when you seek me with all your heart. I will be found by you, declares the Lord" (Jeremiah 29:13–14).

Who may ascend the mountain of the Lord? Who may stand in his holy place? The one who has clean hands and a pure heart, who does not trust in an idol or swear by a false god. They will receive blessing from the Lord and vindication from God their Savior. Such is the generation of those who seek him, who seek your face, God of Jacob.

Psalm 24:3–6

"Seek first his kingdom and his righteousness" (Matthew 6:33).

"Set your minds on things above, not on earthly things" (Colossians 3:2).

"Call to me and I will answer you and tell you great and unsearchable things you do not know" (Jeremiah 33:3).

The Results of Seeking the Lord

Special Relationship with God

There is a relationship with God that is not known without giving yourself to seeking Him. It is an intimate relationship known only between the ones in it. It involves the revealing of one's personality, knowing them for the person they are. God longs for this kind of relationship with us. It is the sharing of secrets known only between close friends. And Jesus shares His secrets with us.

> *Greater love has no one than this: to one lay down one's life for one's friends. You are my friends if you do what I command. I no longer call you servants, because a servant does not know his master's business. Instead, I have called you friends, for everything that I learned from my Father I have made known to you.*

John 15:13–15

There is a close caring for those who are intimate; they care for each other, and this is the care He has for us. There is a concern for the other's well-being as well as a fellowship that is enjoyed with close friends. There is the desire to be with a close friend and the anticipation of time shared together. It is the confidence that if something should happen, my close friend will be with me. Letters are fine when you are not together, but the heart desires to be together.

We have the promise He gave to be with Him forever. "God has said, 'Never will I leave you; never will I forsake you'" (Hebrews 13:5). "Surely I am with you always, to the very end of the age" (Matthew 28:20). It is knowing that He is coming back to take us to be with Him forever.

> *Do not let your hearts be troubled. You believe in God; believe also in me. My Father's house has many mansions; if that were not so, would I have told you that I am going there to prepare a place for you? And if I go to prepare a place for you, I will come back and take you to be with me that you also may be where I am.*

John 14:1–3

I have confidence in knowing that God will always do what is best for me at all times, that He has defeated the enemy, that I am His, and He is mine. It is the giving of myself to another with nothing held back; it is the total opening of myself to Him. There are no secrets held from Him.

Listen to Jesus' promise to this kind of friendship, "You did not choose me; but I chose you and appointed you so that you might go and bear fruit—fruit that will last—and so that whatever you ask in my name the Father will give you" (John 15:16).

Principles for Life

1. God Must Be First in Our Lives

We cannot have anyone or anything that is more important to us than the Lord Himself. He must be Lord of our lives, or He is not Lord at all.

2. When Christ Comes in, Old Things Pass Away

Before we can grow in Him, old things must be replaced with godly principles and character. After Christ comes in, we truly are a new creation.

3. God Directs Our Lives to Bring Us to Himself

All of our steps are ordered by the Lord! There is no coincidence with God; He orchestrates everything in our lives. "The steps of a man are ordered by the Lord" (Psalm 37:23, BSB).

4. God Will Illuminate His Word to Our Hearts

In studying God's Word, He reveals new truths to our hearts.

5. The Word of God Must Be Shared with Others

We are commissioned to share God's Word with others. We are His ambassadors, so be one. Wherever and whenever be prepared to share the Word of God.

6.   God Reveals Himself through His Word

God has planned that through the proclamation of His Word to reveal Himself to us.

7.   New Revelation Results in a New Relationship

With every new revelation about Him, we grow into a new relationship with Him.

CHAPTER EIGHT:
Humiliation

Josiah Humbles Himself before the Lord

When the king heard the words of the Law, he tore his robes. He gave these orders to Hilkiah, Ahikam son of Shaphan, Abdon son of Micah, Shaphan the secretary and Asaiah the king's attendant: "Go and inquire of the Lord for me and for the remnant in Israel and Judah about what is written in this book that has been found. Great is the Lord's anger that is poured out on us because those who have gone before us have not kept the word of the Lord; they have not acted in accordance with all that is written in this book." Hilkiah and those the king had sent with him went to speak to the prophetess Huldah, who was the wife of Shallum son of Tokhath, the son of Hasrah, keeper of the wardrobe. She lived in Jerusalem, in the New Quarter. She said to them, *"This is what the Lord, the God of Israel, says: Tell the man who sent you to me, 'This is what the Lord says: I am going to bring disaster on this place and its people—all the curses written in the book that has been read in the presence of the king of Judah. Because they have forsaken me and burned incense to other gods and aroused my anger by all that their hands have made, my anger will be poured out on this place and will not be quenched.' Tell the king of Judah, who sent you to inquire of the Lord, 'This is what the Lord, the God of Israel, says concerning the words you heard: Because your heart was responsive and you humbled yourself before God when you heard what he spoke against this place and its people, and because you humbled yourself before me and tore your robes and wept in my presence, I have heard you, declares the Lord. Now I will gather you to your ancestors, and you will be buried in peace. Your eyes will not see all the disaster I am going to bring on this place and on those who live here.'" So they took her answer back to the king.*

2 Chronicles 34:19–28

When the king heard the words of the book of the Law, he tore his robes. He gave these orders to Hilkiah the priest, Ahikam son of Shaphan, Akbor son of Micaiah, Shaphan the secretary and Asaiah the king's attendant. "Go and inquire of the Lord for me and for the people and for all Judah about what is written in this book that has been found. Great is the Lord's anger that burns against us because those who have gone before us have not obeyed the words of the book; they have not acted in accordance with all that is written there concerning us." Hilkiah the priest, Ahikam,

Akbor, Shaphan and Asaiah went to speak to the prophetess Huldah, who was the wife of Shallum son of Tikvah, the son of Harhas, keeper of the wardrobe. She lived in Jerusalem, in the New Quarter. She said to them, "This is what the Lord, the God of Israel, says: Tell the man who sent you to me, 'This is what the Lord says: I am going to bring disaster on this place and its people, according to everything written in the book the king of Judah has read. Because they have forsaken me and burned incense to other gods and aroused my anger by all the idols their hands have made, my anger will burn against this place and will not be quenched.' Tell the king of Judah, who sent you to inquire of the Lord, 'This is what the Lord, the God of Israel, says concerning the words you heard: Because your heart was responsive and you humbled yourself before the Lord when you heard what I have spoken against this place and its people—that they would become a curse and be laid to waste—and because you tore your robes and wept in my presence, I also have heard you, declares the Lord. Therefore I will gather you to your ancestors, and you will be buried in peace. Your eyes will not see all the disaster I am going to bring on this place.'" So they took her answer back to the king.

2 Kings 22:11–20

"Neither before nor after Josiah was there a king like him who turned to the Lord as he did—with all his heart and with all his soul and with all his strength" (2 Kings 23:25).

Josiah's Response to the Word of the Lord

Josiah Aligned Himself with the Word of God

Josiah had received the report from the temple repair committee and found that it was going well. He also learned that they found the "Book of the Law" while cleansing the temple. It was found by Hilkiah, the high priest, and given to Shaphan, the secretary of state, who in turn took it to the king and read it to him.

We do not know how much of the Law was read to him before he responded to it. But we do know that he acted in true remorse and with great grieving over the realization of their sin. The Bible says that he tore his robe, a sign of true remorse, and a sign of the rending of his heart for the dishonor done to God. He also wept in sorrow over their failure to obey God's Word. The fact that Josiah responded as he did indicates his acceptance of God's Word as the one and only rule for faith and conduct for his personal life and for the nation of Judah. His response was sincere and genuine and in keeping with the seriousness of the sins committed. May we have the same response as Josiah to sin in our lives. People who will give God's Word a fair hearing, and be honest with themselves, will find that it will bring them to their knees in humble repentance. Unless we "abhor ourselves, and repent in dust and ashes," Scripture has not done its work in us, and all of our reading of it is in vain. May we not become so "familiar" with the Word of God that it becomes just another book to us, and we do not allow the Holy Spirit to bring us under the conviction of sin. May we allow the Holy Spirit to speak to us, convict us, and lead us to repentance.

The apostle James gives the proper response to God's Word:

> *Do not merely listen to the word, and so deceive yourselves. Do what it says. Anyone who listens to the word but does not do what it says is like someone who looks at his face in a mirror and, after looking at himself, goes away and immediately forgets what he looks like. But whoever looks intently into the perfect law that gives freedom, and continues in it—not forgetting what he has heard, but doing it—they will be blessed in what they do.*
>
> **James 1:22–25**

Josiah not only looked at himself through the lens of God's Word but acted accordingly in humiliation, repentance, and obedience. His response to God's Word put him in favor with God; he was rewarded with the promise of peace in his lifetime, and the blessing of the Lord was upon his kingdom.

If we do not humble ourselves before Him in this life, we will, on one day of necessity, bow in humble admission and confess that He is Lord.

> *God exalted Him to the highest place and gave him the name that is above every name, that at the name of Jesus every knee should bow, in heaven and on earth and under the earth, and every tongue acknowledge that Jesus Christ is Lord, to the glory of God the Father.*
>
> **Philippians 2:9–11**

Josiah Did Not Justify Himself

Josiah did not turn his thoughts toward other people's sins but included himself with them in the sin of the nation. For anyone to receive forgiveness for sin, you have to acknowledge that you have sinned and are a sinner. Had Josiah tried to justify himself, he would not have truly been repentant nor received the reprieve that God granted him. Listen to his words:

> *Go and inquire of the Lord for me and for the remnant in Israel and Judah about what is written in this book that has been found. Great is the Lord's anger that is poured out on us because those who have gone before us have not kept the word of the Lord; they have not acted in accordance with all that is written in this book.*

2 Chronicles 34:21

He acknowledged his sin and that of the people. In short, he was saying, "we have sinned."

To receive forgiveness and pardon, you have to acknowledge your sinfulness to God. The Word of God is very clear on this point; all have sinned. Unless we admit we are sinners, we cannot be forgiven. You will never confess to something of which you are not guilty nor aware of. And that brings us to the next step: Had Josiah not received the book of the Law, he would not have humbled himself before God and asked for pardon.

We must proclaim the gospel of Christ to the whole world because all people will be judged by it one day in the presence of God. So, it is imperative that we proclaim the good news. Without the knowledge of the gospel, people won't come to know Him. We must proclaim it so that they will have an opportunity to accept Christ as their Lord and Savior.

Confession is important to forgiveness. The Bible says, "If we confess our sins, he is faithful and just and will forgive us our sins and purify us from all unrighteousness" (1 John 1:9). So, to receive pardon, I must acknowledge my sin and then confess it and ask for His forgiveness. It does me no good to justify myself against others' sins by comparing my "not so bad sins against their flagrant, over the top, willful sins." I must accept the responsibility for my sins and ask God for His cleansing, and He will do it!

Josiah Realized the Disobedience Involved the Entire Nation

Go and inquire of the Lord for me and for the remnant in Israel and Judah about what is written in this book that has been found. Great is the Lord's anger that is poured out on us because those who have gone before us have not kept the word of the Lord; they have not acted in accordance with all that is written in this book.

2 Chronicles 34:21

Their disobedience would not only bring God's wrath upon Josiah but his nation as well. The warning is not only for him as an individual, but for the nation too. The judgment of God would fall upon the nation because the warning had come to them as a nation. Beginning with Moses, Joshua, Samuel, Elijah, Elisha, Isaiah, Zephaniah, and now Jeremiah, as well as many other minor prophets, had proclaimed warning after warning against Israel and Judah for the sins they were committing. The "Word of the Lord" had been given over and over again against their sin and wickedness with no apparent response from the people. They completely ignored the prophets, and in many cases, tortured them or put them to death.

God is a loving, longsuffering God, but He says in His Word, "My Spirit will not contend with humans forever" (Genesis 6:3). The cup of iniquity was full; the judgment of

God would be poured out upon a sinful people. And they would have no excuse. The patience of God had come to an end. Now judgment would come, and it would be all-encompassing. The nation would now experience the consequences of its sinful ways. Except for the godly Josiah, it would have come sooner.

Josiah Sought for Confirmation

Is It True?

The first question that came to Josiah's mind was, "Is it true?" The reason for the question is if it is "great is the Lord's wrath that is kindled against us," then the second follows right after, "When will it happen?" Josiah wanted to know where they stood in relation to the coming judgment.

Josiah didn't hesitate to respond when he heard the Law read. He immediately took action to inquire whether or not it was true. He didn't wait to look into it later, nor did he set up a study committee to investigate the matter. He didn't respond as did Felix, the governor of Judea, when Paul was proclaiming the gospel to him, "That's enough for now! You may leave. When I find it convenient, I will send for you" (Acts 24:25). May the Lord help us to respond as Josiah did when we read His Word.

Unfortunately, there are many people who cannot bring themselves to believe that God would punish well-meaning people. The problem is not that God judges us by our intentions but by our response to the sacrifice of His Son, Jesus. They say, "God is a God of love, and He wouldn't send anyone to hell." And they are right; God doesn't send anyone to hell; they go there by their own choices. He puts all kinds of obstacles in our way so we won't end up in hell, and we have to ignore them to end up there. He makes it quite plain; only by accepting Christ can we have access to the Father.

God's wrath will come upon those who have sinned and not accepted Christ as Savior.

Go, Inquire of the Lord

Obviously, the trusted members of Josiah's cabinet did not have any more information for him because he sent them together as his emissaries to inquire of the Lord for the answers.

Josiah's instructions to the delegation were, "Go and inquire of the Lord for me and for the people...." Josiah wanted to get the answers from the right source. He went to the same place where he started when he began seeking the Lord for himself. He also surrounded himself with godly men who, like himself, wanted to know the truth. You cannot find the truth if you look for it from people who don't have it or to religions that don't know it. The one source for truth is His Word. It can be trusted, and it is proven to be trustworthy. It will lead you into truth. Not only does His Word guide us, but He has also sent His Holy Spirit to lead us into truth. God will respond to a searching heart and reveal His truth to you. He will show it to you because He is not willing for any to perish but that all might come to repentance.

Inquire of the Right Sources

Not only should we look for the truth in God's Word, but His Word warns us where *not to look.* You can't turn to the ungodly when searching for truth. Furthermore, to enquire of a "medium" or "sorcerer" was forbidden by God. Listen to God's Word:

> *"I will set my face against anyone who turns to mediums and spiritists to prostitute himself by following them, and I will cut him off from their*

people" (Leviticus 20:6).

When you enter the land the Lord your God is giving you, do not learn to imitate the detestable ways of the nations there. Let no one be found among you who sacrifices his son or daughter in the fire, who practices divination or sorcery, interprets omens, engages in witchcraft, or casts spells, or who is a medium or spiritist or who consults the dead. Anyone who does these things is detestable to the Lord, because of these detestable practices the Lord your God will drive out those nations before you. You must be blameless before the Lord your God.

Deuteronomy 18:9–13

Not only were they not to inquire of a medium but not to practice it also:

"A man or a woman who is a medium or spiritist among you must be put to death. You are to stone them; their blood will be on their own heads" (Leviticus 20:27).

"Do not practice divination or sorcery" (paraphrased by the author) (See Deuteronomy 18:9–13).

They were to listen only to the prophet of the Lord:

The nations you will dispossess listen to those who practice sorcery or divination. But as for you, the Lord your God has not permitted you to do so. The Lord your God will raise up for you a prophet like me from among you, from your fellow Israelites. You must listen to him.

Deuteronomy 18:14–15

God does not permit His people to be involved with fortune tellers, reading tarot cards and tea leaves, astrology, black magic, white magic, palm reading, familiar spirits, mediums, séance, witches, yoga, zodiac, fetishes, fire walking, hexes, automatic writing, Ouija boards, or astral projection. These are all forbidden by the Lord. Not because He is afraid of competition, or that one will discover something He is trying to keep secret from them. But because there is no other God besides Him and to seek such sources for finding out the future or secrets leaves one open to the deception of the devil.

Satan's job is to deceive you into accepting a lie. He will use any source at his disposal to accomplish that. He did the same thing in the garden with Adam and Eve. His line was, "Did God really say?" (Genesis 3:1), raising a question about God's intentions. And the other line was, "You will be like God, knowing good and evil" (Genesis 3:5).

What Can I Do?

Josiah also wanted to know what he could do about the situation. When we are confronted with God's truth, the natural question is, "What can I do?" In the book of Acts, we read that on the day of Pentecost, after Peter spoke, the question by those who heard was, "Brothers, what shall we do?" (Acts 2:37). And again, in Philippi, the jailer asked Paul and Silas, "What must I do to be saved" (Acts 16:30). The answer is always the same: "Repent."

I believe that our nation is about at the same place as was Judah during Josiah's time. We, too, must humble ourselves and repent or receive the judgment of God (we will discuss this further in another chapter).

As far as Josiah's inquiry into what he could do, the answer was that there wasn't anything he could do. Sin had run its course, and God was now to bring judgment upon the nation. That must have been a very troubling thing for Josiah. As a godly leader, he wanted so much to avert the coming wrath, but that was not to be.

Huldah the Prophetess

Hilkiah the priest, Ahikam, Akbor, Shaphan and Asaiah went to speak to the prophetess Huldah, who was the wife of Shallum son of Tikvah, the son of Harhas, keeper of the wardrobe. She lived in Jerusalem, in the New Quarter.

2 Kings 22:14

One may wonder why they went to Huldah to inquire of the Lord when both Zephaniah and Jeremiah were prophesying at this time? The Bible is silent about this. Some think that perhaps Zephaniah's ministry had run its course, and he was through. As far as Jeremiah is concerned, his ministry was just beginning. Jeremiah had only started just five years before, during the thirteenth year of Josiah's reign (at this time, he was in his eighteenth year). It is very likely that both Zepheniah and Jeremiah were well acquainted with Josiah at this time. Perhaps Jeremiah was out of the area at this time. Perhaps God is showing that He speaks through more than just a few. God uses many different people to bring about His purposes.

The Bible says that her husband, Shallum, was the keeper of the wardrobe. But it is not clear if the wardrobe that they were speaking of was that of the king or that of the high priest in the temple. If it was the priestly garments that her husband was in charge of, then both she and her husband would have been known by Hilkiah, the high priest. If it was the king's wardrobe that he was the keeper of, then she would have been known by both the king and those in his administration. In any event, she was known by them, and her word was trusted by them as from the Lord. Looking at it now from a distance, it is obvious that she was the one who had the Word of God for Josiah.

Thing Revealed to Josiah

Josiah's Unworthiness

Josiah realized his unworthiness in the light of God's holiness. When we realize how unworthy we are, we also realize that we are not worthy to come into God's presence. We must acknowledge that we cannot enter into His presence on our own merits. Isaiah also had a similar experience.

> *In the year that King Uzziah died, I saw the Lord seated on a throne, high and exalted, ...and the train of his robe filled the temple. ... "Woe to me!" I cried, "I am ruined! For I am a man of unclean lips, and I live among a people of unclean lips, and my eyes have seen the King, the Lord Almighty.*
>
> **Isaiah 6:1, 5**

He realized that he was unfit to be in His presence. May we be in awe of the majesty, glory, power, and holiness of our God. Without the covering of the blood of Christ, we could never approach the Lord. It is only because of Christ that we can have an audience with our Holy God. We, too, like Josiah, would weep, bow, and tear our robes in humility in the presence of God, and we, too like Isaiah, would cry, "Woe to me!" We are all unworthy to be in His presence.

Josiah's Sinfulness

Josiah recognized that they deserved the judgment of the Lord. As soon as the Word of God was read to him, he recognized that it was true—they had sinned. He confessed, "We have sinned." Because they had sinned, it was just for them to have the judgment of God upon them. And because we too, like Judah, have sinned, we also deserve the judgment of God upon us. We, too, must bow before Him in humility and seek His forgiveness. Since the punishment for sin is death, we are all worthy of death. I may think that I am all right until I see myself as God sees me. When we see ourselves through His eyes, we recognize that we, indeed, are unworthy. The deception of sin makes us feel that we are all right. But the revelation of God's holiness shows us the true state of our lives. When Josiah heard the Word of God, he cried, "Great is the anger of the Lord that is poured out on us, for we have not kept the words of this book nor the words of the Lord." Oh, how our hearts deceive us. We think that everything is fine until we get a glimpse of how God views us.

There Are Consequences to Sin

Josiah's response was, "Great is the Lord's anger that is poured out on us because those who have gone before us have not kept the word of the Lord; they have not acted in accordance with all that is written in this book."

As soon as he heard the Word of God, Josiah grasped the seriousness of their situation with God. Not only did God say that judgment would come upon sin, but that He was now about to do it. The Bible says, "The one who sins is the one who will die" (Ezekiel 18:4). And that is what Josiah and Judah were about to experience. Somehow, they never seemed to understand that one day there would be a reckoning. They just went on with their lives day after day, expecting that it would be like this until they died. They never understood that God keeps His word. Just as God cast out and destroyed the inhabitants of the land before them because of their wicked ways, so He was now about to do the same to Judah. They went on, oblivious to the imminent danger that was about to befall them. That is the way it is with most people in sin; there seems to be no realization that they will have to give an account of themselves before God.

What Josiah Saw about God

His Word Is True

Josiah's response to the hearing of the Word of God was also a realization that God's Word is true. Somehow humankind has had problems realizing that God says what He means and means what He says. Josiah's request of those he sent to inquire of the Lord was, "Go and inquire of the Lord for me and for the people and for all Judah about what is written in this book that has been found." In other words, "Is it really true? Is the judgment of the Lord truly about to happen to us?" In reading between the lines, it seems as though he was questioning whether or not it was true. But it was true, as Josiah found out. Huldah's answer left no doubt or question:

> *This is what the Lord says: I am going to bring disaster on this place and its people—all the curses written in the book that has been read in the presence of the king of Judah. Because they have forsaken me and burned incense to other gods and aroused my anger by all that their hands have made, my anger will be poured out on this place and will not be quenched.*
>
> **2 Chronicles 34:24–25**

The message for Josiah was: Yes, it is true, and yes, My judgment will be poured out.

The testimony of Abraham reinforces the certainty of God's Word. "[Abraham] was strengthened in his faith and gave glory to God, being fully persuaded that God had power to do what he had promised" (Romans 4:20–21). The thing about the Word of God is that it doesn't matter whether or not His Word is about a promised blessing in obedience to His Word or a promised curse in disobedience to His Word. It is His Word, and it will come true.

His Hatred for Sin

This is what the Lord, the God of Israel, says:
Tell the man who sent you to me, "This is what
the Lord says: I am going to bring disaster on
this place and its people—all the curses written
in the book that has been read in the presence of
the king of Judah. Because they have forsaken me
and burned incense to other gods and aroused my
anger by all that their hands have made, my anger
will be poured out on this place and will not be
quenched."

2 Chronicles 34:23–25

Judah will receive the full force of the wrath of God on their sin. God is serious about sin! He hates sin. His judgment will be poured out on it. The word of the Lord came to Josiah that when it happens, God will not stop it "My anger will be poured out on this place and will not be quenched." May God help us to see how much God hates sin. Our righteous God cannot and will not ignore sin.

God is a holy and righteous God. He cannot co-exist with evil. That is why Satan was removed from His presence. The two of them have nothing in common. He hates sin! There is no compatibility between God and Satan. There is coming a time, according to the Bible, when God will pour out His wrath on this old sinful world. This world will be so traumatized that people will call upon the rocks to fall on them and crush them. Ever since the fall in the garden, God has been dealing with the sin problem, which will continue until Satan is finally put away for good. Then, and only then, we will live eternally in His presence without any fear of retribution for sin, for we will finally be free.

His Determination to Deal with Sin

Huldah's response to their inquiry was short and to the point. Yes, the Word of God is true! And I am going to deal with their sin, and it will be devastating. Or to use a modern term, "It won't be pretty."

The one thing that Josiah came away with from his inquiry into the words of the book was that God was determined to deal with sin and that it could not be put off any longer. Sin cannot be ignored; it cannot be winked at. God cannot let it go without taking action on it; sin must be dealt with. It is a fearful thing to fall into the hands of an angry God (Hebrews 10:31).

There are two ways in God's Word that sin is dealt with:

1. By the way God dealt with it in Old Testament times; the animal sacrificial system to appease God's judgment, or

2. Through the sacrifice of His Son on Calvary's cross, for those who accept His forgiveness and pardon.

There is no other way to heaven; it is only through the blood Christ shed on the cross. "There is no other name under heaven given to mankind by which we must be saved" (Acts 4:12). Christ is the only way to God. In Christ, we have full assurance of sins forgiven and can have peace with God without fear of retribution for any past sins committed. Those who have not dealt with the sin question in their lives will still have to answer to Him for them. Thank God that, through Jesus Christ, we can have full assurance that our sins are taken care of and will never be remembered against us again. It was His great love for humankind that caused Christ to come to earth and settle the sin question for you and me. He did not just give up on us but dealt with it because we were unable to do so ourselves. So, we can say like the Apostle Paul, "Thanks be unto God for His unspeakable gift" (2 Corinthians 9:15, KJV).

What Josiah Experienced

God's Response to a Repentant Heart

When the envoy went to Huldah for answers, she told them,

> *Tell the king of Judah, who sent you to inquire of the Lord, "This is what the Lord, the God of Israel, says concerning the words you heard: Because your heart was responsive and you humbled yourself before God when you heard what he spoke against this place and its people, and because you humbled yourself before me and tore your robes and wept in my presence, I have heard you, declares the Lord.*
>
> **2 Chronicles 32:26–27**

When Josiah inquired of the Lord, God was there to hear and answer him. The answer was not all that he wanted it to be, but there was mercy shown to Josiah for his repentant heart. The sins of the nation had gone to the point of no return as far as God's judgment was concerned. But the assurance for Josiah was that God had heard him and given him the answer he was looking for—the truth.

It is also true today; all who will call upon Him shall be saved because He is not willing that any should perish but that all may come to repentance and forgiveness (2 Peter 3:9). Praise God that He still hears the prayer of a repentant sinner and will freely pardon us.

God's Protection from Judgment

*Tell the king of Judah, who sent you to inquire of
the Lord, "This is what the Lord, the God of Israel,
says ..., I also have heard you, declares the Lord.
Therefore I will gather you to your ancestors, and
you will be buried in peace. Your eyes will not see
all the disaster I am going to bring on this place"
So they took her answer back to the king.*

2 Kings 22:18–20

The one thing about this passage is that it is both tragic
and hopeful; tragic for Judah and hopeful for Josiah. How
tragic that the nation had put off dealing with their sin and had
to go through this devastating, horrible experience that would
totally devastate the country and leave many people broken,
disillusioned, in poverty, and under a cruel foreign ruler.

On the other hand, because of his responsive repentant
heart Josiah:

1. Was heard by God.

2. Was given a response from God.

3. Was protected from the coming judgment.

4. Lived out his life in peace (under no foreign rule).

5. Lived out his life free to worship God in His
   temple in accordance with the Law.

6. Lived free from a guilty conscience.

7. "Was gathered to his grave in peace" (before the
   judgment fell).

As for today, we too have the promise of God that we will
not have to endure the wrath of God that He will pour out
on those who have rejected Him. Instead of hearing, "Depart
from me, ye that work iniquity" (Matthew 7:23, KJV). We

will hear, "Well done, good and faithful servant! ... Come and share you master's happiness!" (Matthew 25:21). We to will be spared God's wrath and judgment that will come upon a sinful world.

God's Approval of Josiah's Actions

The fact that God heard him, answered his request, gave him a life of peace, and blessed him was the reward for Josiah seeking after God. He had the confidence that God approved of his conduct and that he had a heart for God. The blessings that Josiah received, and the peace of mind, far outweighed any inconvenience that he experienced along the way in his effort to know God. The fact that there was opposition to his reforms goes without saying, but it is interesting that the Bible doesn't dwell on those who opposed him but on the positive reforms that he accomplished. It is obvious that they did oppose him because immediately after he was killed in battle, they went right back to their wicked ways and worshiped other gods. Too many people dwell on the fight to get where they are and do not appreciate what they have achieved. Josiah didn't dwell on the hard-fought battles, only on the positive results.

Another evidence of God's approval of Josiah is the fact that there is a great amount of space in the Bible taken up with the life of Josiah. God would not have given so much space to recognize someone who was not His follower and disciple. The story of his life is recorded in 1 Kings, 2 Kings, 2 Chronicles, and as well many of the prophets refer to him in their writings. The abundant record is a wonderful testimony to God's approval of his life.

Too Little, Too Late

Judgment Will Come

The report from the prophetess Huldah declared,

> *This is what the Lord, the God of Israel, says: Tell the man who sent you to me, "This is what the Lord says: I am going to bring disaster on this place and its people—all the curses written in the book that has been read in the presence of the king of Judah. Because they have forsaken me and burned incense to other gods and aroused my anger by all that their hands have made, my anger will be poured out on this place and will not be quenched.*
>
> **2 Chronicles 34:23–25**

I believe that our nation needs to take a warning from this story. We must humble ourselves before God and ask for His forgiveness, for if God's judgment fell on Judah, it will happen to us for the same reasons.

But Not in Your Lifetime

> *Because your heart was responsive and you humbled yourself before God when you heard what he spoke against this place and its people, and because you humbled yourself before me and tore your robes and wept in my presence, I have heard you, declares the Lord. Now I will gather you to your ancestors, and you will be buried in peace. Your eyes will not see all the disaster I am going to bring on this place and on those who live here.*
>
> **2 Chronicles 36:27–28**

Within just twenty-three years after Josiah's death, Judah and Jerusalem came to an end and went into exile to Babylon just as God's prophets had prophesied.

Perhaps we, too, will have a stay of God's judgment if we humble ourselves and call on Him for mercy. Oh, God, may it be so!

Principles for Life

1. Josiah Sought for Divine Confirmation

We, too, must go to the right source for the right answers.

2. Josiah Surrounded Himself with Godly Counselors

Those from whom you seek advice will determine what course you will take.

3. Josiah Had a Passion for Righteousness

Jesus said, "Blessed are those who hunger and thirst for righteousness, for they will be filled" (Matthew 5:6).

4. Josiah Realized That God's Word Is True

> *The Lord Almighty has sworn, "Surely, as I have planned, so it will be, and as I have purposed, so it will happen. ...The Lord Almighty has purposed, and who can thwart him? His hand is stretched out, and who can turn it back?*

Isaiah 14:24, 27

5. Josiah Realized That Sin Affects Everyone

> *Great is the Lord's anger that is poured out on us because those who have come before us have not kept the word of the Lord; they have not acted in accordance with all that is written in this book.*

2 Chronicles 34:20

6. Josiah Humbled Himself before the Lord

"Humble yourself before the Lord, and he will lift you up" (James 4:10).

7. Josiah Realized That God Hates Sin

Those who sin will die!

8. Josiah Learned That God Responds to a Repentant Heart

"If we confess our sin, he is faithful and just and will forgive us our sins and purify us from all unrighteousness" (1 John 1:9).

CHAPTER NINE:
Proclamation

Josiah Proclaims the Word to the People

The king called together all the elders of Judah and Jerusalem. He went up to the temple of the Lord with the people of Judah, the inhabitants of Jerusalem, the priests and the Levites—all the people from the least to the greatest. He read in their hearing all the words of the Book of the Covenant, which had been found in the temple of the Lord. The king stood by his pillar and renewed the covenant in the presence of the Lord—to follow the Lord and keep his commands, statutes and decrees with all his heart and all his soul, and to obey the words of the covenant written in this book. Then he had everyone in Jerusalem and Benjamin pledge themselves to it; the people of Jerusalem did this in accordance with the covenant of God,

183

the God of their ancestors. Josiah removed all the detestable idols from all the territory belonging to the Israelites, and he had all who were present in Israel serve the Lord their God. As long as he lived, they did not fail to follow the Lord, the God of their ancestors.

2 Chronicles 34:29–33

Then the king called together all the elders of Judah and Jerusalem. He went up to the temple of the Lord with the people of Judah, the inhabitants of Jerusalem, the priests and the prophets—all the people from the least to the greatest. He read in their hearing all the words of the Book of the Covenant, which had been found in the temple of the Lord. The king stood by the pillar and renewed the covenant in the presence of the Lord—to follow the Lord and keep his commands, statutes and decrees with all his heart and all his soul, thus confirming the words of the covenant written in this book. Then all the people pledged themselves to the covenant.

2 Kings 23:1–3

"Neither before nor after Josiah was there a king like him who turned to the Lord as he did—with all his heart and with all his soul and with all his strength" (2 Kings 23:25).

King Josiah Receives the Word of God

Josiah Had to Decide What to Do with God's Word

Josiah, like everyone else who hears the Word of God, was responsible for what he heard. Once it was confirmed for him by Huldah that God's Word was true, the next question for him was, "What am I going to do with it?" He had received the report from the prophetess Huldah which confirmed his suspicions that God's judgment was going to come on the nation, but it also included a postscript: "It will not happen in your lifetime." It was good news for Josiah, but what about the people? Since they are going to have to endure God's judgment, some may wonder, why not just eat, drink, and be merry for tomorrow we die?

Fortunately, that is not the way Josiah chose to respond. He chose to heed God's warning for himself and to share what he had learned with the people. Perhaps they, too, will repent and turn to God, and, maybe, the Lord would look down on them and spare them too. He would do what he could and leave the rest in God's hands.

Josiah chose to hear, heed, and obey the Word of God for himself and, as much as possible, encourage the same for his nation. He realized that, for too long, they had ignored God's Word and were suffering the consequences for it. The same is true for us today. When we hear the Word of God, we too must decide what we are going to do with it. To heed and obey the Word will mean God's blessing upon our lives, but to ignore and disobey it means we will suffer His wrath and judgment.

He Chose to Read God's Word to the People

The king called together all the elders of Judah and Jerusalem. He went up to the temple of the Lord with the people of Judah, the inhabitants of Jerusalem, the priests and the Levites—all the people from the least to the greatest. He read in their hearing all the words of the Book of the

Covenant, which had been found in the temple of the Lord.

2 Chronicles 34:29–30

What is interesting here is that Josiah chose to read the Word of God to the people. He did not gather them together to make a speech and draw attention to himself. He read the Law to them and drew their attention to the God of Israel. How different that is than many leaders today who gather their people to make speeches and appear to be the Savior. The other striking thing about this event is that "he read in their hearing all the words of the Book of the Covenant." He could have ordered the high priest to do it, but it was so important to him that he did it. May God give us leaders whose main priority is to bring the nation back to God and live according to the principles of the Word.

Josiah's choice was to read it before the people. This news was so great, so important, so awesome, so frightening, so dreadful, and so directed at them that everyone needed to hear it. Though it affected Josiah greatly, it affected the people more. They must know the peril they are in so they can repent.

Because God's Word is all-encompassing, we must take the great commission seriously as the church of Christ and proclaim it to the world. The world must hear so they can make a decision to follow Christ.

But that decision must start with each individual first. I trust that when you hear God's Word, you will choose, as did Josiah, to heed and obey it. Then, in turn, teach and impart it to your children so they too can follow in your footsteps and follow Christ.

It is imperative that we choose to respond as King Josiah did and share the Word of God with family, friends, acquaintances as well as others God would bring across our pathway.

Josiah Read All the Words of the Book

"He read in their hearing all the words of the Book of the Covenant, which had been found in the temple of the Lord" (2 Kings 23:2).

Josiah did not pick and choose what portions of God's Word he was going to read; he read it all. He wasn't concerned about hurting people's feelings. At this point, they were all under the judgment of God. The only hope was for the nation to wholly turn to God in repentance, and perhaps God would reconsider His severe punishment and give them favor. It was not for Josiah to decide which portions were appropriate and which ones were not. It was God's Word! Josiah's responsibility was to read it to them. Their responsibility was to accept it and act accordingly. The people were responsible for what they heard. But they could not make a proper decision without knowing what the truth was. They had to have it all to be able to properly decide to obey.

God's Word is not just one-sided; He gives us both the blessings and the benefits of obeying His Word, as well as the punishment and judgments for disobeying His Word. What Josiah read to the people was the total Law, not just the curses. He read it all, which contained both blessings and curses. When it was read to the people, they realized that they had been living in disobedience to it and, therefore, were now deserving of His curse and judgment.

It is the same today. We are conveyors of truth, and that includes *all* the Word of God. It is the ministry of the Holy Spirit to convict of sin and bring people to repentance. We are to proclaim God's Word fearlessly and let the Holy Spirit do His work in their lives—and He will! When the people have the Word of God, they are able and will make a choice, one way or another.

Josiah Went Up to the House of the Lord

"He went up to the temple [house] of the Lord" (2 Chronicles 34:30).

No place could be more suitable for the reading of the Word of God, and the renewing of the covenant between God and His people, than the house of the Lord. This was the place where the priests and people met with God, so it was only appropriate that they should also hear His Word read there. The people had a great history of meeting with God in the tabernacle in the wilderness and now the temple in Jerusalem. So likewise, it was fitting that they hear God's message to them at the temple. For them, this was like holy ground, a place where God speaks to His people.

May we, today, have that same sense of coming into His presence when we enter our churches and have that same reverence for God and His Word. We sing the song, "We Are Standing on Holy Ground," and may we have that sense that truly we are standing on holy ground as we come into His house and hear His Word read. The words of the chorus "In the Presence of Jehovah" should reflect our devotion as we come into His house:

> *In the presence of Jehovah,*
> *God almighty, Prince of peace,*
> *Troubles vanish, hearts are mended,*
> *In the presence of the King.*

The Martins,
"In the Presence of Jehovah"

May ministers not be ashamed to open and read God's Word to the people. We are bombarded with so much in the world it is refreshing to hear God's Word and have a word from the Lord. May we cherish, reverence, and respect God's Word, not only in the hearing of it but also in the application of it to our daily lives.

The King Read the Word to the People

Josiah Called the Elders Together

"Then the king sent and gathered together all the elders of Judah and Jerusalem" (2 Chronicles 34:29).

The elders were those who were magistrates and representatives in the local government, the political leaders of the people. It was imperative for them to hear and know what God was saying to the nation. Those in leadership needed to know what God was saying to their nation. They also needed to know how dire and serious their situation was. For them to know, they had to hear and understand God's Word. There could be no proper direction for those in leadership without the knowledge of God's Word.

Likewise, today, those in leadership must know what God's Word says so they can effectively lead us in righteousness. How I thank God for godly men and women who are involved in our political system. We must hold them up in prayer as they are a minority in our government.

May those in leadership make the Word of God a priority in their lives so they can effectively give direction and leadership to our nation.

The Men of Judah Were There

"He went up to the temple of the Lord with all the people of Judah" (2 Chronicles 34:30).

In Jewish culture, it was the men who were the leaders both politically and in the home. Without the men behind him, Josiah would not have been able to bring about any reformation, and they would still be under the judgment of God. Men were key to bringing about any change within the country.

The importance of men leading our homes today is of the utmost importance. At a time when we have fatherless homes and absentee fathers, from not only homes but families, we must get back the formula of God's Word and have godly, caring, involved, loving fathers who recognize their true position in their home and will take the lead in the reading and application of the Word of God. Children need to have the example of a godly father to follow and pattern their lives after. Men need to step up and take their rightful place in the home and lead their family in worship, service, and commitment to God. But if the father will not take his rightful place, then the mother must step up and do it in his place. It is not worth it to let your children end up without a relationship with God. God give us men who will do it!

The Priests, the Levites, and the Prophets Were There

The king called together all the elders of Judah and Jerusalem. He went up to the temple of the Lord with the people of Judah, the inhabitants of Jerusalem, the priests and the Levites (2 Chronicles 34:30). Second Kings 23:2 mentions the prophets were there too.

The priests and the Levites dealt with the facilities and sacrifices involved in the temple worship. They were the caretakers of the sacred things in the temple. They represented the people to God and God to the people. The prophets were those who spoke for God and gave His message to the people. Josiah wanted to make sure that those who ministered in these areas would not only hear the Word but be aware of the coming pronounced judgment.

Those who handle the Word and work in His house are held to a higher standard simply because of the position they hold. There is perhaps no higher calling than to proclaim His eternal Word. God helps us so that our continual working with His Word and in His house would not cause us to take it lightly or have a casual attitude about it. If we preach the Word of life, we must also know the bread of life. In his letter to Timothy, Paul warns about those who become so familiar with the Word that the Word loses its value and importance to us. "Having a form of godliness but denying its power" (2 Timothy 3:5).

This is Paul's charge to those who preach the Word of life:

> *In the presence of God and of Christ Jesus, who will judge the living and the dead, and in view of his appearing and his kingdom, I give you this charge: Preach the word; be prepared in season and out of season; correct, rebuke and encourage—with great patience and careful instruction. For the time will come when people will not put up with sound doctrine. Instead, to suit their own desires, they will gather around them a great number of teachers to say what their itching ears want to hear. They will turn their ears away from the truth and turn aside to myths. But you, keep your head in all situations, endure hardship, do the work of an evangelist, discharge all the duties of your ministry.*
>
> **2 Timothy 4:1–5**

Just because people do not want to hear the truth does not exempt us from proclaiming it. We are still required to faithfully proclaim it fearlessly, boldly, and with the power of the Holy Spirit's anointing. God give us men and women of God who will, without hesitation or shame, declare the whole counsel of God.

All the People Were There

"He went up to the temple of the Lord with the people of Judah, the inhabitants of Jerusalem, the priests and the Levites—all the people from the least to the greatest" (2 Chronicles 34:30).

Josiah realized that the Word of God was for everyone. It was not just for him, the elders, and the men, but it was for everyone. He summoned a general assembly of the people. The Bible says they all went to Jerusalem from the least to the greatest. He did not leave anybody out; it was for everyone. He didn't differentiate between classes, race, gender, education, or social standing; he brought them all to hear God's Word. The entire city turned out to hear the Word of God read.

The gospel of Christ is for everyone, and just as Josiah did not leave anyone out, we cannot do so either. The "good news" is for everyone; the up-and-outer as well as the down-and-outer. We cannot differentiate between people either because they are all in the same category anyway—they are all lost and in need of a Savior. If we don't tell them, who will? For God is not willing that any should perish, but that all should come to repentance. Whosoever will come. The great commission includes everyone, "Go into all the world and preach the good news to all creation. Whoever believes and is baptized will be saved, but whoever does not believe will be condemned" (Mark 16:15–16).

May God burden our hearts for those who are unreached from the gospel of Christ. There are so many who have not yet heard. We live at a time when with modern travel and technology, the world is within our reach. We have no excuse for not sharing the good news with the whole world. If it is impossible for us to go with the gospel, we can give so others can go, and our reward will be just as great as theirs will be.

The Response to the Word of God

Josiah Renews the Covenant

The king stood by his pillar and renewed the covenant in the presence of the Lord—to follow the Lord and keep his commands, statutes and decrees with all his heart and all his soul, and to obey the words of the covenant written in this book.

2 Chronicles 34:31

Josiah Stood by His Pillar

Evidently, there was a place within the temple grounds where formal national ceremonies were conducted. Some contend that there was a porch of pillars where this took place. Others state that it was a platform where Josiah stood, and others think he stood on the platform of the bronze laver within the courtyard of the temple. All of them believe that it was a raised platform of some kind that stood above the level of the people. In any event, it seems as though this was a place where formal public national events took place before the people. It was fitting for the king to make this national call to renew the covenant with the people there.

Josiah Led the Way

The king stood by his pillar and renewed the covenant in the presence of the Lord—to follow the Lord and keep his commands, statutes and decrees with all his heart and all his soul, and to obey the words of the covenant written in this book.

2 Chronicles 34:31

King Josiah personally responded to the Word of God in the presence of the Lord and in the sight of the people. The king set the example. He covenanted to keep it all, not just the parts of it that felt good to him. This was a total commitment on his part he agreed to:

1. Follow the Lord

2. To keep His commandments, statutes and His decrees

3. To do it with all his heart, with all his soul

4. To obey the words of the covenant written in the book

This was a very serious commitment for Josiah. It was not a halfway thing with him. He was totally committed to do it. He would obey explicitly, not just when he felt like it or when it was popular or when it was convenient. Josiah gave himself to the pledge.

Whenever the Word of God is read, there will be a response to it. Your response will be to either hear and obey, or you will hear and disregard it. Jesus deals with our response to the Word of God in His sermon on the mount, in the parable of the wise and foolish builders. Jesus likens those who hear and obey to the man who hears the Word and obeys it to the man who built his house upon the rock. And He likens those who hear the Word and disobey it to the man who built his house upon the sand. When the storm came, the house on the rock stood firm, but the house on the sand crumbled into the sand (Matthew 7:24–27).

When we gather together in the Lord's house to worship, praise, glorify and bless His name, or hear the Word of the Lord, whether read, preached, or taught, we bear a personal responsibility to obey what we have heard. Jesus said, "Where two or three gather in my name, there am I am with them" (Matthew 18:20). In other words, He is a witness to what was said and the covenants made. We must remember it is God whom we are dealing with, not people. I don't have to please anyone but God.

The People Pledged Themselves to the Covenant.

"Then he had everyone in Jerusalem and Benjamin pledge themselves to it; the people of Jerusalem did this in accordance with the covenant of God, the God of their ancestors" (2 Chronicles 34:32).

Josiah called the people to join with him in making a covenant with God. He would ask them to make the same commitment that he did. He would not ask them to do something that he would not also commit to himself.

In the light of history, we see that this obedience only lasted as long as Josiah was alive. But I believe that, at the time they did it, they were sincere in their commitment. They did it because it was the Word of God. They did it because God spoke to them. They did it because of their history. Their parents and grandparents had done it. They did it because King Josiah led the way and set an example for them.

What you do in relation to the Word of God is more

important than you may realize. There are those who are watching your life and the way you live. May you live in such a way as to positively affect right choices in the lives of those you are mentoring and for whom you set an example. Happy is the man whose children will follow in his footsteps in committing their lives to God because their father set the example. The English Revised Version reads, "He caused all that were in Jerusalem and Benjamin to stand to it." And they did it! The impact and value of a godly example is priceless. God give us more men like Josiah.

The Results of the Commitment

Josiah removed all the detestable idols from all the territory belonging to the Israelites, and he had all who were present in Israel serve the Lord their God. As long as he lived, they did not fail to follow the Lord, the God of their ancestors.

2 Chronicles 34:33

Revival Spread throughout the Land

As a result, the nation made several positive changes: First, all idolatry was done away within the land. This was not only in the nation of Judah but also in the northern kingdom belonging to Israel. Second, all who were present in Israel began again to serve the Lord. Third, as long as Josiah lived, they continued to follow the Lord, the God of their fathers. This reformation in Judah and Jerusalem happened in Josiah's eighteenth year. He reigned for thirty-one years, and so for thirteen years, the people lived in a state of revival in the land following this event.

The life of Josiah speaks to the importance of the example

of godly leaders. People follow leadership, both good and bad. We have examples of both. Examples of bad leadership include Adolf Hitler, Saddam Hussain, Jim Jones, and David Koresh. Some examples of good leadership include George Washington, Abraham Lincoln, Martin Luther, James Hudson Taylor, David Livingston, D. L. Moody, and George Mueller. Each one of these affected the lives of their followers in powerful, dramatic, and in some cases, devastating ways.

Principles for Life

1. God's Word Is for Everyone

Josiah read in their hearing all the words of the Book of the Covenant, which had been found in the temple of the Lord.

2. God's Word Must Be Received in Its Entirety

Josiah read it all to the people. "All scripture is God-breathed and is useful for teaching, rebuking, correcting and training in righteousness so that the servant of God may be thoroughly equipped for every good work" (2 Timothy 3:16).

3. God's Word Was Read in the Temple

Our place of worship must be a place where we can hear the Word of God.

4. Josiah Set the Example for the People

Those in leadership must commit themselves to follow the Lord.

> *The king stood by his pillar and renewed the covenant in the presence of the Lord—to follow the Lord and keep his commands, statutes and decrees with all his heart and all his soul, and to obey the words of the covenant written in this book.*

2 Chronicles 34:31

5. When Godly Leaders Lead, the People Will Follow

"The people of Jerusalem did this in accordance with the covenant of God, the God of their ancestors" (2 Chronicles 34:32).

6. When People Turn to God, Revival Follows

"Josiah removed all the detestable idols from all the territory belonging to the Israelites, and he had all who were present in Israel serve the Lord, the God of their ancestors" (2 Chronicles 34:33). When people turn to God, it has social implications: Crime rates fall, abuse declines, relationships are restored and strengthened, and God is honored.

CHAPTER TEN:

Return to Holiness

The Celebration of the Passover

*Josiah celebrated the Passover to the Lord
in Jerusalem, and the Passover lamb was
slaughtered on the fourteenth day of the first
month. He appointed the priests to their duties
and encouraged them in the service of the Lord's
temple. He said to the Levites, who instructed all
Israel and who had been consecrated to the Lord:
"Put the sacred ark in the temple that Solomon son
of David king of Israel built. It is not to be carried
about on your shoulders. Now serve the Lord your
God and his people Israel. Prepare yourselves
by families in your divisions, according to the
instructions written by David king of Israel and
by his son Solomon. Stand in the holy place with a*

group of Levites for each subdivision of the families of your fellow Israelites, the lay people. Slaughter the Passover lambs, consecrate yourselves and prepare the lambs for your fellow Israelites, doing what the Lord commanded through Moses. Josiah provided for all the lay people who were there a total of thirty thousand lambs and goats for the Passover offerings, and also three thousand cattle—all from the king's own possessions. His officials also contributed voluntarily to the people and the priests and Levites. Hilkiah, Zechariah and Jehiel, the officials in charge of God's temple, gave the priests twenty-six hundred Passover offerings and three hundred cattle. Also Konaniah along with Shemaiah and Nethanel, his brothers, and Hashabiah, Jeiel and Jozabad, the leaders of the Levites, provided five thousand Passover offerings and five hundred head of cattle for the Levites. The service was arranged and the priests stood in their places with the Levites in their divisions as the king had ordered. The Passover lambs were slaughtered, and the priests splashed against the altar the blood handed to them, while the Levites skinned the animals. They set aside the burnt offerings to give them to the subdivisions of the families of the people to offer to the Lord, as is written in the Book of Moses. They did the same with the cattle. They roasted the Passover animals over the fire as prescribed, and boiled the holy offerings in pots, caldrons and pans and served them quickly to all the people. After this, they made preparations for themselves and for the priests, because the priests, the descendants of Aaron, were sacrificing the burnt offerings and the fat portions until nightfall. So the Levites made preparations for themselves and for the Aaronic priests. The musicians, the descendants of Asaph, were in the places prescribed by David, Asaph, Heman and Jeduthun the king's seer. The gatekeepers at each gate did not need to leave their posts, because their fellow Levites made the preparations for them. So at that time the entire service of the Lord was carried out for the celebration of the Passover and the offering of burnt offerings on the altar of the Lord, as King Josiah had ordered. The Israelites who were present celebrated the Passover at that time and observed the Festival of Unleavened Bread for seven days. The Passover had not been observed like this in Israel since the days of the prophet Samuel; and none of the kings of Israel had ever celebrated such a Passover as did Josiah, with the priests, the Levites and all Judah and Israel who were there with the people of Jerusalem. This Passover was celebrated in the eighteenth year of Josiah's reign.*

2 Chronicles 35:1–19

The king gave this order to all the people: "Celebrate the Passover to the Lord your God, as it is written in this Book of the Covenant." Not since the days of the judges who led Israel nor in the days of the kings of Israel and the kings of Judah had any such Passover been observed. But in the eighteenth year of King Josiah, this Passover was celebrated to the Lord in Jerusalem. Furthermore, Josiah got rid of the mediums and spiritists, the household gods, the idols and all the other detestable things seen in Judah and Jerusalem. This he did to fulfill the requirements of the law written in the book that Hilkiah the priest had discovered in the temple of the Lord.

2 Kings 23:21–24

Introduction

The great Passover celebration is the last event in the reign of Josiah that is recorded in God's Word, except for his death. Josiah was a man whose life was lived for the glory of God. As a result of that commitment, God's blessing was on his life, his kingdom, and his subjects. His thirty-one years as their king was a time of blessing and returning to following and worshiping God. But it was also a time of bitter struggle against sin, wickedness, idolatry, and godlessness. Sin and evil do not go away willingly or easily. The worship of other gods was so ingrained in the people, their lives, and their worship that it was a time of great effort to bring it about.

All of these events—the cleansing and restoration of the temple, the finding of the Book of the Law, the public reading of God's Word, the call of consecration back to the Lord, and this celebration of the Passover—happened in the eighteenth year of his reign. Josiah was the most serious of all of the kings of Judah to serve God with his whole heart and soul. He did it with passion and enthusiasm and involved the priesthood, the Levites, and the people. The text which we are using throughout this study is the key to Josiah's success as a godly king: "Neither before nor after Josiah was there a king like him who turned to the Lord as he did—with all his heart and with all his soul and with all his strength" (2 Kings 23:25).

The success of this Passover Feast and the great participation of the people was a testimony to Josiah's commitment and persistence to totally serve the Lord.

There were some factors that contributed to the great national celebration of the Passover, which brought about this mass Passover celebration.

Godly Leaders Commanded It

Josiah Commanded the People to Celebrate the Passover

"The King gave the order to all the people: "Celebrate the Passover to the Lord your God, as it is written in the Book of the Covenant" (2 Kings 23:21).

"So at that time the entire service of the Lord was carried out for the celebration of the Passover and the offering of burnt offerings on the altar of the Lord, as King Josiah had ordered" (2 Chronicles 35:16).

Under Josiah's leadership and example, the people had just pledged themselves to keep the covenant of the Lord. The king stood by his pillar and renewed the covenant in the presence of the Lord,

> *To follow the Lord and keep his commands, statutes and decrees with all his heart and all his soul, and to obey the words of the covenant written in this book. Then he had everyone in Jerusalem and Benjamin pledge themselves to it; the people of Jerusalem did this in accordance with the covenant of God, the God of their ancestors.*
>
> **2 Chronicles 34:31–32**

So, it was fitting for them to take the next step and celebrate the Passover Feast. This was the feast that was initiated in Egypt and commanded by God for them to keep yearly as a reminder of what God had done for them in delivering them from slavery in Egypt. In essence, what Josiah was saying was, "Now that you have agreed to keep the covenants of the Lord, let's do it!" Josiah made no apologies for ordering them to follow through with their commitment to obey the covenant. To him, it was only natural that they take the next step and keep the Passover.

Josiah was not from the priestly (religious) line but was from the kingly (civil government) line. But he was so convicted by the reading of the Word that he took it upon himself to order obedience to the Word of God. May God raise up godly leaders today who will, with the same determination and zeal, give themselves to serve the Lord with all their heart, soul, and strength.

Josiah Set the Example for the People

Josiah celebrated the Passover to the Lord in Jerusalem (2 Chronicles 35:1).

Josiah personally celebrated the Passover with the people. This became so important to him that he not only kept the Passover for himself, but he provided Passover animals for the people, many of whom could not afford a lamb. Josiah provided for all the lay people who were there (a total of thirty thousand sheep and goats for the Passover offerings, and also three thousand cattle) all from the king's own possessions (2 Chronicles. 35:7).

He set the example for them to follow. It is one thing to say, "You need to do this." But it is another to set an example for others to follow. When leaders lead by example, people will follow. God places great importance on the conduct of leadership. There are those who say that your private life and your public life are two different things, but that's not what God says. The way you live in your private life will dictate how you will live in your public life. "Such a person is double-minded and unstable in all they do" (James 1:8). Character is important when choosing a leader. If you cannot be faithful in the little things, how can you be faithful in greater areas? The way you live impacts everyone around you. Sin hurts everybody, not just yourself. Jesus said in the sermon on the mount,

> *You are the salt of the earth. But if the salt loses its saltiness, how can it be made salty again? It is no longer good for anything, except to be thrown out and trampled underfoot. You are the light of the world. A town built on a hill cannot be hidden. Neither do people light a lamp and put it under a bowl. Instead they put it on its stand, and it gives light to everyone in the house. In the same way, let your light so shine before others, that they may see your good deeds and glorify your Father in heaven.*

Matthew 5:13–16

May God give us godly men and women who will be examples in government, the church, and their homes.

Josiah's example led others to follow him in what he did. They, too, donated sacrificial animals for the Passover Feast. His officials also contributed voluntarily to the people as well as the priests and Levites.

> *Hilkiah, Zechariah and Jehiel, the officials in charge of God's temple, gave the priests twenty-six hundred Passover offerings and three hundred cattle. Also Konaniah along with Shemaiah and Nethanel, his brothers, and Hashabiah, Jeiel and Jozabad, the leaders of the Levites, provided five thousand Passover offerings and five hundred head of cattle for the Levites.*

2 Chronicles 35:8–9

Very often, when one takes the initiative and does something, it encourages others to also follow the Lord in that same way. As a result, many are used, and God is glorified.

Josiah Did Away with Sin and Unrighteousness

He got rid of everything that represented idolatry and godlessness. He removed all the detestable idols from all the territory belonging to Israel. Josiah thoroughly cleansed the land, both Judah and Israel, of idolatry (2 Chronicles 34:33a).

Josiah not only did away with the practice of heathen worship, but he also got into their private lives as well. "Josiah got rid of the mediums and spiritists, the household gods, the idols and all the other detestable things seen in...Jerusalem" (2 Kings 23:24).

If the Word of God is to be effective at all, it must be effective in our home life. Our children must see godly examples in our homes by their parents so they, in turn, can pass it on to their children.

One other important note here is that the cleansing of the land preceded the celebration of the Passover Feast. It is imperative that our lives be cleansed prior to our celebration in worship. God always deals with sin first, and then He pours out His blessing on us. The whole premise of forgiveness is preceded by repentance, and then forgiveness follows. If we confess our sins, He is faithful and just to forgive us our sins (1 John 1:9). Sin must be done away with. May God help us to understand how much He hates sin. The two cannot cohabit together. That is what repentance is all about. Conversion is not adding Christianity along with other forms of worship but forsaking them and serving only the one true God.

He Did It to Please God

Josiah got rid of the mediums and spiritists, the household gods, the idols and all the other detestable things seen in Judah and Jerusalem. This he did to fulfill the requirements of the law written in the book that Hilkiah the priest had discovered in the temple of the Lord.

2 Kings 23:24

King Josiah cleansed the land to fulfill the requirements of the book. He was so intent on pleasing his God that he wasn't concerned about hurting the feelings of those living in sin. After all, they were going to come under God's judgment for those very sins. I am sure that there were those who were offended by him. But it is better to please God than gain the praise of people. It is *His* approval that is important. It is God who said that these practices were detestable.

The People Were Eager to Respond

The People Were Ready for Revival

The people had come with Josiah through the finding of the Law to the reading of the Law, and finally to a commitment to serve the Lord their God. The next step was to participate in the worship and celebration of the most important of their feasts—the Passover.

For nearly six decades given themselves to worshiping pagan heathen gods, but the opportunity to give themselves wholly in worship to God was now theirs. They had all heard about this great feast, and now they would participate in it. Josiah was the first king in many decades to provide the opportunity for this celebration. The incentive to worship, the opportunity to worship, the atmosphere for worship—all were in place, and they responded with eager participation.

What a difference a righteous king makes for his subjects.

Instead of being ordered to worship other gods, they were now being ordered to worship the God of their fathers, the one the Book of the Law told them about, which was found in the temple. The difference in the attitude of the people when the wicked rule and the godly is mentioned in Proverbs, "When the wicked rise to power, people go into hiding; but when the wicked perish, the righteous thrive" (Proverbs 28:28). "When the righteous thrive, the people rejoice; when the wicked rule, the people groan" (Proverbs 29:2). Wicked leaders rule through fear and subjugation, but the righteous rule through kindness and love. The people of Israel had been under wicked rulers and now were experiencing the wonderful freedom of living under a caring and thoughtful ruler. When godly rulers lead, the people will follow.

All Were Invited to Participate

"The king gave this order to all the people: 'Celebrate the Passover to the Lord your God, as it is written in this Book of the Covenant'" (2 Kings 23:21).

"And Israel who were present there with the people of Jerusalem" (2 Chronicles 35:18).

When Israel was taken captive by the Assyrians, the people were deported and sent to different countries to prevent them from uprising and rebellion. But the people who remained in the territory of Israel were all invited to participate in the Passover Feast. The context suggests that many of them took advantage of the opportunity and came to Jerusalem to participate with Josiah and Judah.

Josiah invited all who were in Israel, from the northern ten tribes, to join in the celebration, and many came to Jerusalem. There were those who were true to the worship of God down through the decades and were eager to be part of the new thing that God was doing under Josiah.

Wherever God's Word has been proclaimed, there are those who believe and remain faithful in their commitment to God.

Everything Was in Its Proper Place

1. The Passover Kept in the First Month

> *"Josiah celebrated the Passover to the Lord in Jerusalem, and the Passover lamb was slaughtered on the fourteenth day of the first month" (2 Chronicles 35:1).*

> *The Lord said to Moses and Aaron in Egypt, "This month is to be for you the first month, the first month of your year. Tell the whole community of Israel that on the tenth day of this month each man is to take a lamb for his family, one for each household. ...The animals you choose must be year-old males without defect, and you may take them from the sheep or the goats. Take care of them until the fourteenth day of the month, when all the members of the community of Israel must slaughter them at twilight. Then they are to take some of the blood and put it on the sides and tops of the doorframes of the houses where they eat the lambs. That same night they are to eat the meat roasted over the fire, along with bitter herbs, and bread made without yeast. ...On the same night I will pass through Egypt and strike down every firstborn of both men and animals, and I will bring judgment on all the gods of Egypt. I am the Lord. The blood will be a sign for you on the houses where you are, and when I see the blood, I will pass over you. No destructive*

plague will touch you when I strike Egypt. This is a day you are to commemorate; for the generations to come you shall celebrate it as a festival to the Lord—a lasting ordinance.

Exodus 12:1–3, 5–8, 12–14

Josiah ordered the Passover to be kept on the proper date for it, the fourteenth day of the first month. This was unlike the great Passover Feast celebrated by King Hezekiah, who, because it had not been kept for some time, had it celebrated in the second month. Josiah was doing everything in accordance with the Book of the Law.

2. The Ark of the Covenant Returned to Its Place

He said to the Levites, who instructed all Israel and who had been consecrated to the Lord: "Put the sacred ark in the temple that Solomon son of David king of Israel built. It is not to be carried about on your shoulders."

2 Chronicles 35:3

There is no explanation with this passage as to why they were carrying the ark of the covenant around on their shoulders. There is only speculation as to why that was so:

a. The ark had been taken out of its proper place in the Holy of Holies while they were doing the repair work ordered by King Josiah and was not yet replaced;

b. The ark had been removed by King Manasseh to make room for the heathen gods which he worshiped and was never replaced;

c. The ark had been removed by the priests for safekeeping under the rule of Manasseh and Amon and not replaced;

d. The ark was carried about and used as a good luck object.

Another reason for having the ark in the temple was to free up the priests who were carrying it, so they could now give themselves to the duties prescribed for them and carry out their duties during the Passover Feast.

3. The Burnt Offerings Were Offered on the Altar

"So at that time the entire service of the Lord was carried out for the celebration of the Passover and the offering of burnt offerings on the altar of the Lord, as King Josiah had ordered" (2 Chronicles 35:16).

The Book of the Law contained specific instructions for the offering of burnt sacrifices and offerings, and Josiah made every effort to have the priests follow every detail in accordance with those instructions. The altar probably had not been used in its proper manner for some time, possibly, since Hezekiah's reign.

4. The Utensils Used for the Sacrifices

"They roasted the Passover animals over the fire as prescribed, and boiled the holy offerings in pots, caldrons and pans and served them quickly to all the people" (2 Chronicles 35:13).

There were utensils crafted for the priests to use in the offering of sacrifices to the Lord. It was the responsibility of the priests and Levites to keep them ready for use for this purpose. It was important that everything be in its proper place so the Passover Feast could be carried out efficiently and orderly. This was especially so on this occasion when there were so many animals for them to deal with.

There is an important lesson for us here. We are reminded

that there is a lot of detailed work that must be carried out in preparation for the work of the Lord to go forth. If you find yourself in a mundane, no glory, behind-the-scenes position and wonder if anyone notices, be confident that the God who ordered these mundane jobs to be performed is aware of your labor.

God does not reward on the prestige of the task, but according to faithfulness. The parables of the servants who were given money to put into use were all about faithfulness. The admonition for them was "Well done good and faithful servant" (see Matthew 25:14–30). The servant who hid his talent was called a "wicked and lazy servant." The faithful servant was received into God's kingdom, and the other was thrown out into everlasting darkness. We are to be faithful servants. Many times, it involves doing tedious, mundane chores. Paul also deals with faithfulness in our service: "It is required that those who have been given a trust must prove [trustworthy] faithful" (1 Corinthians 4:2).

Everyone Functioned in Their Assigned Place

1. The Priests and the Levites

He appointed the priests to their duties and encouraged them in the service of the Lord's temple. "...Now serve the Lord your God and his people Israel. Prepare yourselves by families in your divisions, according to the directions written by David king of Israel and by his son Solomon. Stand in the holy place with a group of Levites for each subdivision of the families of your fellow Israelites, the lay people. Slaughter the Passover lambs, consecrate yourselves and prepare the lambs for your fellow Israelites, doing what the

Lord commanded through Moses." The service
was arranged and the priests stood in their places
with the Levites in their divisions as the king had
ordered. The Passover lambs were slaughtered,
and the priests splashed against the altar the
blood handed to them, while the Levites skinned
the animals. They set aside the burnt offerings to
give them to the subdivisions of the families of
the people to offer to the Lord, as is written in the
Book of Moses. They did the same with the cattle.

2 Chronicles 35:2–6, 10–12

This was to be a joint effort with both the priests and the Levites. To accomplish the task before them, they had to work together. The priests sprinkled the blood on the altar, and the Levites skinned the animals, and then they gave them to the people who were to eat portions of the sacrificed animals. The task before them was very demanding in that they had to slaughter over 41,000 animals in sacrifice, a task which took them all day. There were certain responsibilities for the priests and specific responsibilities for the Levites to perform. Each one had to function where they were assigned to accomplish the task.

God has a place for each one of us in the body of Christ. Be content to function where He has placed you. You will be rewarded accordingly. Do your job faithfully and leave your brother or sister to the Lord. He knows what is best for them.

2. The Musicians Were in Their Place

"The musicians, the descendants of Asaph, were in
the places prescribed by David, Asaph, Heman and
Jeduthun the king's seer" (2 Chronicles 35:15).

From the beginning of the church, music has been a foundational and crucial component of worship. Worship is often expressed with spontaneous worship in music (both instrumental and vocal) from the heart. Music prepares the heart and the mind to receive from the Lord. The musicians involved here at the Passover Feast utilized both instrumental and vocal music. Music is a very effective means of presenting the gospel of Christ. It was important then, and it is important today.

3. The Porters Were in Their Place at the Gates

"The gatekeepers at each gate did not need to leave their posts, because their fellow Levites made the preparations for them" (2 Chronicles 35:15).

There were Levites who stood by the gates and took the sacrificed portions to the people so they could participate in the festival. With so many people involved, there would be no room for them all within the temple complex. The porters took their positions by the gates, serviced the people, and kept order within the temple grounds.

4. All Done in Proper Order

"So at that time the entire service of the Lord was carried out for the celebration of the Passover and the offering of burnt offerings on the altar of the Lord, as King Josiah had ordered" (2 Chronicles 35:16).

When everyone is functioning in their proper place, everything is done in unity and harmony. Everyone is included, no one is left out, and God is glorified. No wonder it was a time of great celebration.

God's Blessing Was upon the Celebration

God Was in His Rightful Place

Under Josiah's watchful eye, the temple had been renovated and restored, the temple worship was once again resumed, daily ministry was carried out by the priesthood, the ark of the covenant was put back in its rightful place, the Passover was kept by the people, and the nation had turned back to God. The important factor was that God was once again part of their thinking, worship, and national life. When God is in His proper place in the life of a nation, then His blessing will follow. God cannot bless what He is not a part of. "Blessed is the nation whose God is the Lord" (Psalm 33:12).

The admonition of the Lord to King Solomon is fulfilled here for Josiah and Judah:

> *If my people, who are called by my name, will humble themselves and pray and seek my face and turn from their wicked ways, then will I hear from heaven, and will forgive their sin and will heal their land. Now my eyes will be open and my ears attentive to the prayers offered in this place.*
>
> **2 Chronicles 7:14–15**

That is what happens when we obey and follow Him. God honors His Word, and His blessing follows.

Everything Was in Accordance with the Word of God

> *"The king gave this order to all the people: 'Celebrate the Passover to the Lord your God, as it is written in this Book of the Covenant'"* (2 Kings 23:21).

215

Prepare yourselves by families in your divisions, according to the directions written by David king of Israel and by his son Solomon. ...Slaughter the Passover lambs ...and prepare the lambs ...doing what the Lord commanded through Moses. They set aside the burnt offerings to give them to the subdivisions of the families of the people to offer to the Lord, as it is written in the Book of Moses.

2 Chronicles 35:4, 6, 12

Josiah was determined to do everything according to the Book of the Law. We, too, must come to the point where what we do is "according to the Word of the Lord." There can be no mistake for us; we have the Word of God, and we must do it. Paul admonishes us, "Be very careful, then, how you live—not as unwise but as wise. ... Therefore do not be foolish, but understand what the Lord's will is" (Ephesians 5:15, 17).

The Feast of Unleavened Bread Lasted for Seven Days

"The Israelites who were present celebrated the Passover at that time and observed the Festival of Unleavened Bread for seven days" (2 Chronicles 35:17).

The Feast of Unleavened Bread followed the Passover Feast and lasted for seven days.

For seven days you are to eat bread made without yeast. On the first day remove the yeast from your houses, for whoever eats anything with yeast in it from the first day through the seventh must be cut off from Israel. On the first day hold a sacred assembly, and another one on the seventh day. Do no work at all on these days, except to prepare food for everyone to eat; that is all you may do.

Celebrate the Festival of Unleavened Bread, because it was on this very day that I brought your divisions out of Egypt. Celebrate this day as a lasting ordinance for the generations to come.

Exodus 12:15–17

The Passover Feast and the Festival of Unleavened Bread were to be celebrated back-to-back as prescribed by Moses in Egypt. The Passover Feast and the Festival of Unleavened Bread were linked together in the deliverance of Israel from Egypt. Both had great significance for the Israelites. On this occasion, the people celebrated them both with great passion and active participation.

Nothing Like This Before nor After

"Neither in the days of the judges who led Israel nor in the days of the kings of Israel and the kings of Judah had any such Passover been observed" (2 Kings 23:22).

The Passover had not been observed like this in Israel since the days of the prophet Samuel; and none of the kings of Israel had ever celebrated such a Passover as did Josiah, with the priests, the Levites and all Judah and Israel who were there with the people of Jerusalem.

2 Chronicles 35:18

There was not a Passover Feast like this before Josiah nor following. This particular Passover Feast was so special that it is recorded in Scripture as such. No other Passover Feast could compare with it in scope, participation, solemnity, and spiritual fervor.

There were a series of events, in a very precise order that was followed which brought the renewal about:

1. There was an acute hunger for the Word of God.

2. There was the return to the Word of God.

3. There was the cleansing of their lives from any form of sin.

4. There was the making of a new covenant between the people and the Lord.

5. When all of these were accomplished, it was only natural to give yourself in worship to the Lord.

Today we would call this a "revival." People turned away from sin and a self-satisfying lifestyle to one of forsaking sin and returning to the worship of the Lord. This kind of "revival" has its effects on our national life, our community life, our family life, and our religious life. May God grant us such a revival in our day that people will turn so whole-heartedly unto the Lord in commitment, worship, and devotion.

Principles for Life

1. Revival Does Not Just Happen

Certain things must be in place for Revival to occur. In Josiah's case, all those things fell into place:

a. The leaders promoted and encouraged it.

b. Many of the people in both Judah and Israel were ready, willing, and hungry for it.

c. The blessing of the Lord was upon it.

2. They Followed Strict Instructions for It

The guidelines for the Passover Feast were outlined for them in the Book of the Law. Josiah was very careful to observe and follow all the requirements written there.

3. **The Great Celebration Included and Involved Everyone**

It included the king and his administration, the priests, the Levites, the musicians, the city officials, and all the people, and many from Israel.

4. **It Happened After They Turned Whole-Heartedly to God**

The revival had to be preceded by total denunciation of all heathen gods and worship.

5. **It Was a Time of Great Rejoicing and Celebration**

"Neither in the days of the judges who led Israel nor in the days of the kings of Israel and the kings of Judah had any such Passover been observed"
(2 Kings 23:22).

6. **God Was Restored to His Rightful Place**

When we place the Lord where He belongs, there is peace, harmony, contentment, and the blessings of God.

CHAPTER ELEVEN:
Josiah's Untimely End

Josiah Is Killed in Battle

After all this, when Josiah had set the temple in order, Necho king of Egypt went up to fight at Carchemish on the Euphrates, and Josiah marched out to meet him in battle. But Necho sent messengers to him, saying, "What quarrel is there, king of Judah, between you and me? It is not you I am attacking at this time, but the house with which I am at war. God has told me to hurry; so stop opposing God, who is with me, or he will destroy you." Josiah, however, would not turn away from him, but disguised himself to engage him in battle. He would not listen to what Necho had said at God's command but went to fight him on the plain of Megiddo. Archers shot King Josiah, and he told

*his officers, "Take me away; I am badly wounded."
So they took him out of his chariot, put him in
his other chariot and brought him to Jerusalem,
where he died. He was buried in the tombs of his
ancestors, and all Judah and Jerusalem mourned
for him. Jeremiah composed laments for Josiah,
and to this day all the male and female singers
commemorate Josiah in the laments. These became
a tradition in Israel and are written in the Laments.
The other events of Josiah's reign and his acts of
devotion in accordance with what is written in the
Law of the Lord—all the events, from beginning to
end, are written in the book of the kings of Israel
and Judah.*

2 Chronicles 35:20–27

*Now the rest of the acts of Josiah, and all that
he did, are they not written in the book of the
chronicles of the kings of Judah. In his days
Pharaoh-nechoh king of Egypt went up against
the king of Assyria to the river Euphrates: and
king Josiah went against him; and he slew him at
Megiddo, when he had seen him. And his servants
carried him in a chariot dead from Megiddo, and
brought him to Jerusalem, and buried him in his
own sepulcher.*

2 Kings 23:28–30 (KJV)

*"Neither before nor after Josiah was there a king
like him who turned to the Lord as he did—with
all his heart and with all his soul and with all his
strength" (2 Kings 23:25).*

The Last Thirteen Years of Josiah's Reign

The Silence of Scripture

The main thrust of the historians of 2 Kings and 2 Chronicles was to chronicle Josiah's search for the true God of Israel, the righteous reforms he undertook, his reading of the Scriptures to the people, the call to covenant with God to serve Him all their days, and the celebration of the great Passover Feast. These indeed were the highlights of the reign of King Josiah. After these were recorded, Scripture is silent on the next thirteen years of his reign.

The events of Josiah's reign from his eighteenth to his thirty-first year are left blank, both in the account in 2 Kings and 2 Chronicles. "Josiah appears to have conducted himself prudently, gradually extending his power over Samaria and Galilee, without coming into hostile collision with any of the neighboring nations" (*The Pulpit Commentary*. Vol. 12, 2 Kings, page 450).

We can assume that Josiah never lost his fervor in serving the Lord, that his kingdom continued to expand to include most of the territory of Samaria and Galilee and included the people in the temple worship and offering of sacrifices. It must have been a time of great peace and prosperity, for when people turn back to God, His blessings and provisions are the results. "When the Lord takes pleasure in anyone's way, he causes their enemies to make peace with them" (Proverbs 16:7).

The Changing World Scene

During these thirteen years, things were changing politically.

> *The great invasion of Western Asia by the Scythian*
> *hordes (which is alluded to by Jeremiah 6:1–5 and*
> *Ezekiel 38, 39 and perhaps by Zephaniah 2:6) as*

*also the attack of Psamatik I upon Philistia, the
fall of the Assyrian empire and the destruction of
Nineveh; the establishment of the independence of
Babylon, and her rise to greatness; together with
the transfer of power in the central part of Western
Asia, from the Assyrians to the Medes.*

The Pulpit Commentary

Vol. 12, 2 Kings, pages 449–450

Were all taking place during these last years of Josiah's reign.

Josiah was in a very fast-changing political climate but was unable to accept what was happening, and in the end, it was fatal for him. Josiah was a vassal king under the Assyrians. With their power weakening, Josiah was granted more freedom to expand his kingdom over Samarian and Galilee. He probably didn't want that to change and so opposed King Neco of Egypt.

The Fatal Battle

Neco King of Egypt Attacks Assyria

*"After all this, when Josiah had set the temple
in order, Necho king of Egypt went up to fight at
Carchemish on the Euphrates, and Josiah marched
out to meet him in battle" (2 Chronicles 35:20).*

Interestingly, this is the only battle into which Josiah had ever led his army. He was not a warrior king, but a king given to reformation and turning the people's hearts back to God. This, his only battle, was his end. He was killed in battle.

Nineveh, the capital of Assyria, had already fallen, and King Neco was passing through Judah with his army to Carchemish on the Euphrates River to join up with the

Assyrians against the rising Babylonian empire.

> *Neco King of Egypt: Neco II ascended the throne of the Pharaohs in B.C. 612, and reigned sixteen years. A warlike and adventurous prince, he was likewise devoted to commercial pursuits; he possessed two fleets of Greek-made triremes, one in the Mediterranean and another in the Red Sea. In his service Phoenician sailors were the first to circumnavigate Africa.*
>
> **The Pulpit Commentary**
> **Vol. 14, 2 Chronicles, pages 436–437**

Josiah Positions His Army to Oppose Neco

> *But Neco sent messengers to him, saying, "What quarrel is there, king of Judah, between you and me? It is not you I am attacking at this time, but the house with which I am at war. God has told me to hurry; so stop opposing God, who is with me, or he will destroy you."*
>
> **2 Chronicles 35:21**

As King Neco approached with his army, Josiah with his army confronted him. Neco, Pharaoh of Egypt, sends an envoy to Josiah to inform him that he is not there to attack Judah but that he is on a mission from God to go up to Carchemish to do battle with Assyria against the upstart Babylonian nation. The phrase "the house with which I am at war" was a direct reference to the Babylonians: Nabopolassar was on the throne of Babylon, while his son Nebuchadnezzar was commanding the armies in the field. Nebuchadnezzar would succeed his father after another battle at Carchemish against Egypt in 605 BC (Study Bible, footnote on 2 Chronicles 35:21).

> *Josiah, however, would not turn away from him, but disguised himself to engage him in battle. He*

would not listen to what Necho had said at God's command but went to fight him on the plain of Megiddo.

2 Chronicles 35:22

The historian of Chronicles indicates that the reply of King Neco was really a warning from God. We recall earlier that when confronted with the Book of the Law found in the temple, Josiah sent representatives to Huldah to inquire of the Lord to see whether or not the warning of imminent judgment was really true. But on this occasion, he relied on his own wisdom, and it proved fatal for him. Josiah followed the example of King David in his commitment to the Lord, except in this area of going to war. For when David was confronted with a battle, he consulted the Lord. "Shall I go up against him? Will you grant us victory?" (see 1 Samuel 30:7–9).

It is true that very good men make very great mistakes, and it was true in Josiah's case.

God's Word is silent on the reasoning of Josiah in opposing Necho's army in battle. Perhaps Josiah was reasoning that with Assyria weakening, he would lose the freedom he was experiencing because of Assyria's waning kingdom, and any victory by them would bring them back under stricter and harsher servitude.

Josiah Is Killed in Battle

Archers shot King Josiah, and he told his officers, "Take me away; I am badly wounded." So they took him out of his chariot, put him in his other chariot and brought him to Jerusalem, where he died.

2 Chronicles 35:23–24a

Josiah disguised himself and engaged in battle. The archers shot at him (probably a random shot), hitting him with a mortal strike. He ordered his servants to disengage and retreat from the battle. They brought him to Jerusalem and there he died. Pharaoh Necho then marched his army up to Assyria and joined forces with the Assyrians, and together, they crossed the Euphrates River and lay siege to Harran. The combined forces failed to capture the city, and Necho retreated back to northern Syria.

Josephus Account of the Battle

Flavius Josephus, the Jewish historian, gives this account of the battle:

> *Now Neco, King of Egypt, raised an army, and marched to the river Euphrates, in order to fight with the Medes and Babylonians, who had overthrown the dominion of the Assyrians, for he had a desire to reign over Asia. Now when he was come to the city of Mendes, which belonged to the Kingdom of Josiah, he brought an army to hinder him from passing through his own country, in his expedition against the Medes. Now Neco sent a herald to Josiah, and told him that he did not make this expedition against him, but was making haste to Euphrates; and desired that he would not provoke him to fight against him, because he obstructed his march to the place whither he had resolved to go. But Josiah did not admit of this advice of Neco, but put himself into a position to hinder him form his intended march. I suppose it was fate that pushed him on this conduct, that it might take an occasion against him; for as he was setting his army in array, and rode about in his chariot, from one wing of his army to another, one*

of the Egyptians shot an arrow at him, and put an end to his eagerness of fighting, for being sorely wounded, he commanded a retreat to be sounded for his army, and returned to Jerusalem, and died of that wound.

The Life and Works of Flavius Josephus
Book 10, chapter 5, page 305

Josiah's Final End

Josiah Laid to Rest in Jerusalem

They took him out of his chariot, put him in his other chariot and brought him to Jerusalem, where he died. He was buried in the tombs of his ancestors, and all Judah and Jerusalem mourned for him. Jeremiah composed laments for Josiah, and to this day all the male and female singers commemorate Josiah in the laments. These became a tradition in Israel and are written in the Laments.

2 Chronicles 35:24–25

"And his servants carried him in a chariot dead from Megiddo, and brought him to Jerusalem, and buried him in his own sepulcher" (2 Kings 23:30a, KJV).

Even though Josiah was a godly king, he ignored the warning given him through Neco, king of Egypt, and suffered the consequences. The tragedy of Josiah's life was in the way he died. After having served the Lord faithfully for thirty-one years, how foolish to die when he was so young, age thirty-nine, when he had so many years still ahead of him and all because of one bad mistake in judgment.

His life should be a warning to us not to let down our guard or forsake the Word of the Lord. We cannot take God for granted just because we have lived for Him for a long time. God, keep us faithful to Your Word and an open heart to Your Spirit.

All Judah and Jerusalem Mourned for Him

"Josiah was laid to rest in the tomb of his ancestors" (2 Chronicles 35:24). (This is important because the ungodly kings were not buried in the tombs of their fathers.)

All Judah and Jerusalem mourned for him. Josiah was well-loved by his people. There are not many kings in which the Bible notes that the people mourned for them. But Josiah was an extraordinary young man and one that was loved by his subjects. When godly leaders die, they are mourned by the people, but when the wicked rulers die, there is a sense of relief. "The name of the righteous is used in blessings" (Proverbs 10:7).

Josiah's Son, Jehoahaz, Anointed King

The people of the land took Jehoahaz the son of Josiah and anointed him and made him king in the place of his father. Jehoahaz was twenty-three years old when he became king, and he reigned in Jerusalem three months. His mother's name was Hamutal daughter of Jeremiah; she was from Libnah.

2 Kings 23:30b–31

Then the people of the land took Jehoahaz the son of Josiah and made him king in Jerusalem in place of his father. Jehoahaz was twenty-three years old when he became king, and he reigned in Jerusalem three months.

2 Chronicles 36:1–2

After Josiah's death, the people took Jehoahaz and made him king. His reign lasted only three months. Second Kings 23:32 tells us that king Johoahaz did that which was evil in the sight of the Lord.

> *"[King Neco] took Jehoahaz and carried him off to Egypt, and there he died" (2 Kings 23:34b).*

> *The king of Egypt made Eliakim, a brother of Jehoahaz, king over Judah and Jerusalem and changed his Eliakim's name to Jehoiakim. But Necho took Eliakim's brother Jehoahaz and carried him off to Egypt.*

> **2 Chronicles 36:4**

His reign was short-lived, and he was carried away captive into Egypt and died there.

There Was No King Like Josiah

> *"Neither before nor after Josiah was there a king like him who turned to the Lord as he did—with all his heart and with all his soul and with all his strength" (2 Kings 23:25).*

We have come to the end of this study in the life of King Josiah. Truly, the verse above is a testament to this man who ruled in Judah and to his commitment to serve God with all his heart, soul, and strength.

Even though he was opposed by many in Judah, he was also loved because he was a godly king. When the righteous rule, the people rejoice, but when the wicked rule, the people groan.

Parallels in Josiah's Life and Our Walk with God

Following is a summary of the parallels between Josiah's life and our own walk with the Lord:

First, there were those who were influential in Josiah's life; his mother, Jedidah, the high priest, Hilkiah, and possibly his maternal grandfather in turning his heart toward the Lord. So, too, in our lives, there are those who were instrumental in influencing us to serve the Lord.

Second, Josiah came to the point in his life when he had to know for himself what he believed, and he gave himself to seeking the Lord. Likewise, in our lives, we come to the place where we must know for ourselves and begin to inquire of the Lord and make the faith ours, so we own it.

Third, once Josiah found out that what he learned was true, he acted on that knowledge and took action against those who worshiped other gods; he cleansed the land. In our lives, once we know the truth, we must act accordingly, declare ourselves, and take a stand against unrighteousness.

Fourth, Josiah began to repair the temple and restore temple worship and committed himself to serve the Lord. In doing so, they found the lost Book of the Law. In our lives, we, too, follow these steps in succession.

Fifth, when the Book of the Law was found and read to him, Josiah discovered a new revelation about the God he was now serving, which alarmed him. In our walk with God and study of His Word, we too receive increasing revelation about the Lord and His expectations of us.

Sixth, what Josiah learned humbled him and caused him to repent, with great sorrow, for the sin of his people. In our lives, the more we learn about the Lord, the more we realize how unworthy we are, and we, too, must humble ourselves.

Seventh, what Josiah learned was so important—God's judgment was about to fall upon them—that he was compelled to proclaim it to the people and bring them back into a covenant relationship with the Lord. Likewise, for us, when we realize that those without Christ are lost for eternity, we too must proclaim to them the eternal consequences of their sin and offer the only hope, Jesus Christ.

Eighth, once everything was back in the right relationship with God, it was only natural to celebrate their return to holiness. They celebrated a Passover Feast like no other. In our lives, we, too, can celebrate when our children, family, friends all know the Lord as their Savior.

Principles for Life

1. Don't Get Caught Up in Causes Not Your Own

When we interject ourselves in the cause of another that we should not be in, we do so at our own peril.

2. Don't Reject Good Advice

Josiah should have listened to the advice he received from King Neco.

3. God Uses Ungodly People to Accomplish His Plans

Even though King Neco was not a godly king, God had a plan and purpose for his battle with Assyria.

4. Just because God Has Blessed Us in the Past Is No Assurance of His Continued Blessing

I must seek Him for my present circumstance, not just assume He will be with me now because He was in the past.

5. The Godly Are Honored at Death

Josiah was buried in the tombs of his fathers, and all Judah and Jerusalem mourned for him.

6. One Mistake Can Have Tragic Consequences

There are times when we may not have another chance.

7. The Righteous Are Held in Memory

Jeremiah composed laments for Josiah, and to this day all the male and female singers commemorate Josiah in the laments. These became a tradition in Israel and are written in the Laments.

2 Chronicles 35:25

8. Make Jesus Lord of Your Life

I cannot end this study without extending to you the opportunity to make Jesus Lord of your life. God's Word says, "If we confess our sins, he is faithful and just and will forgive us our sins and purify us from all unrighteousness" (1 John 1:9). He loves you; He died in your place, so you won't have to; He wants you to live with Him for all eternity; His plans for your life will fulfill everything you would ever hope for.

So, pray this prayer with me that will bring you into a personal relationship with God: Jesus, I acknowledge that I am a sinner and need Your forgiveness. I ask You now to forgive me of my sin and make me Your child. Be the Lord of my life and direct my steps from this day forward. Amen.

CHAPTER TWELVE:
America on the Brink

Warning for the Nation

If my people, who are called by my name, will humble themselves and pray and seek my face and turn from their wicked ways, then will I hear from heaven, and will forgive their sin and will heal their land.

2 Chronicles 7:14

Introduction to the Next Two Chapters

During my studies in the life of Josiah, the Spirit of the Lord began to deal with me about this great country of ours. The United States of America has been blessed by the Lord beyond any other nation in modern history. As I observed what is happening in our nation, I was struck by the similarities of the conditions and conduct of the people of the US and that of Judah. As a result, I have gained some insights that I believe are applicable to us today.

One of the reasons for the judgment of God upon Judah was that she forsook the Lord and gave herself to the worship of idols and other forbidden practices that God said were "an abomination to Him." Manasseh led the people astray, so that they did more evil than the nations the Lord had destroyed before the Israelites (2 Kings 21:9). God gave the children of Israel the ten commandments as a guide and direction for their lives and conduct. There are two of the commandments that I want to emphasize which highlight practices that God has forbidden:

First: They were to have no other gods before Him; they were not to make any graven images, nor were they to bow down before them or worship them.

There was good reason for God to give this command: *It was true; there really were no gods to compare to Him!* This was not only true because He said it, but He proved to them that it was true. The mighty manifestation of His power and glory on their behalf was repeated over and over again. From their deliverance from Egypt and their wanderings in the wilderness to His mighty power when they went into the promised land to possess it, there was a constant reminder of His power, majesty, and intervention on their behalf. God also let them know what the blessings would be if they obeyed and what the penalty would be if they were to disobey these commands. If they obeyed, His blessings would be upon them to one thousand generations, but if they disobeyed, His curse would be upon them to the third and fourth generation (Exodus 20:4–6). Israel never understood the anger of the Lord that they generated when they worshipped other gods. And the seventy years of captivity was about a three generations span.

Second: They were not to practice any of the abominable acts of worship of the nations around them, and all the things God forbid were included in their pagan worship.

The worship of Baal, the god of the Philistines, and Molech, the god of the Canaanites, were particularly forbidden because they both included temple prostitution and child sacrifices. In the case of Baal worship, the priests of Baal and the priestesses of Asherah would have sexual intercourse as part of their worship, and the child produced by that union would then be offered in sacrifice on the altar of Baal. In the case of the worship of Molech, the same scenario was true, and the child was burned in sacrifice to the god of Molech. During the ceremony, they would beat drums to obscure the screams and cries of the children being burned to death in sacrifice. These practices were one of the reasons for God's command to destroy them as a people.

This brings me to a striking similarity between Josiah's time and ours. Although today we in America do not bow before graven images, we still worship gods other than the Lord. Today, we sacrifice our children on the altar of abortion as we bow to the gods of convenience, lust, pleasure, and irresponsibility. Here are some facts about abortion: More innocent human beings are put to death every day than those who died in the 9/11 attack, 3,000. Abortion ends the lives of more than 1.5 million unborn children in America every year. Over 15 percent of all pregnancies end in abortion. (The overwhelming majority of those innocent children are simply sacrificed on the altar of convenience.) Between fifty-five and sixty million unborn babies have been murdered by abortion since the Supreme Court ruling on January 22, 1973.

Opinion: America on abortion

More than 80 percent of Americans believe legal abortion should be either prohibited or limited, according to a new survey. The poll of US adults shows:

Eleven percent support a total ban on abortion.

Thirty-eight percent favor restricting abortion to cases of rape, incest, or a threat to the life of the mother.

Thirty-three percent endorse limiting the procedure to the first three or six months of pregnancy.

Only 9 percent favor unlimited abortion rights through abortion.

Startling Statistics

I heard these statistics on the radio—Focus on the Family:

Of all the children conceived in 2000,

- Twenty-five percent were aborted
- Thirty-five percent were born to unwed parents
- Today in the US, 50 percent will not reach age sixteen before their parents' divorce
- Only one in four will live their lives with both parents

Dr. Dobson indicates that "based on these trends in the census, about half of the children today will spend at least part of their childhood in single-parent homes." That's one out of two! We are moving swiftly toward a traditional post-family society.

This brings us face to face with a startling reality: If God would pour out His judgment on His chosen people for their sins, then He would do the same against us for ours. The slaughter of innocent children was a major factor in God's judgment on Israel and Judah and, I am convinced that the slaughter of innocent children in America will also bring about the judgment of God upon the US.

There were certain reasons for God's judgment given in the history of Judah, and they are outlined. There were also certain criteria for God to delay His judgment, and those also are given. My prayer is that we may humble ourselves and seek the Lord; perhaps He will give us a stay from His judgment.

Reasons for God's Judgment

The Cup of Iniquity Is Full

Continual Disobedience to God's Will Bring Judgment

> *Great is the Lord's anger that is poured out on us because of those who have gone before us have not kept the Word of the Lord; they have not acted in accordance with all that is written in this book.*

2 Chronicles 34:21

Manasseh's sin brought God's judgment on Judah, God said,

> *I am going to bring such disaster on Jerusalem and Judah that the ears of everyone who hears of it will tingle. I will stretch out over Jerusalem the measuring line used against Samaria and the plumb line used against the house of Ahab. I will wipe out Jerusalem as one wipes a dish, wiping it and turning it upside down. I will forsake the remnant of my inheritance and give them into the hands of enemies. They will be looted and plundered by all their enemies; they have done evil in my eyes and have aroused my anger.*

2 Kings 21:12–15

Even after Josiah humbled himself before the Lord, it still wasn't enough to avert the judgment of God.

> *Nevertheless, the Lord did not turn away from the heat of his fierce anger, which burned against Judah because of all that Manasseh had done to arouse his anger. So, the Lord said, "I will remove Judah also from my presence as I removed Israel, and I will reject Jerusalem, the city I chose, and this temple, about which I said, 'My Name shall be there.'"*

2 Kings 23:26–27

God is a God of patience and long-suffering, but there comes a time when even God says, "Enough is enough!" Down through history, we have seen those times as recorded in the Bible. He has declared, "My Spirit will not contend with humans forever" (Genesis 6:3). In the Old Testament, we saw it at the time of the flood, at the tower of Babel (Genesis 11:1–9), with Sodom and Gomorrah (Genesis 18:20–19:26); we saw it time and again with His chosen people Israel. Finally, we saw it when He sent them into captivity in Babylon. When iniquity has reached its limit, then God's wrath will be poured out on sin. When people do not obey the Word of the Lord, rest assured, at some point, He will pour out His judgment on them. Ignorance is not a viable excuse for mercy. God holds us accountable for what He has said. We must know and obey His commands!

Continual forsaking of God to worship other gods by His people brings a response from Him,

> *This is what the Lord says: I am going to bring disaster on this place and its people—all the curses written in the book ...because they have forsaken me and burned incense to other gods and aroused*

my anger by all that their hands have made.

2 Chronicles 34:24–25

Judah could not say that God had not warned them. He sent them prophet after prophet to warn them and plead with them to return to Him, but they either ignored them, persecuted them, or murdered them.

When Josiah sent the delegation to inquire of the Lord through Huldah, this is what she told him. The sin of the people has become too great. To put it in modern terminology, it was "Too little, too late."

We see an example of this in the story of the flood,

> *The Lord saw how great man's wickedness of the human race had become on the earth, and that every inclination of the thoughts of the human heart was only evil all the time. The Lord regretted that he had made human beings on the earth, and his heart was deeply troubled. So the Lord said, "I will wipe from the face of the earth the human race I have created ...for I regret that I have made them."*

Genesis 6:5–7

Just as the Lord did not turn away from the heat of His fierce anger against mankind at the time of the flood or Judah for her sin, so the Lord will also pour out His judgment today for our sin. There is a time when God's mercy, patience, and long-suffering come to an end, and judgment must fall upon sin.

God's Warning to a Sinful Nation

The Lord said, "My Spirit will not contend with humans forever, for they are mortal" (Genesis 6:3). The time of God's patience is nearly over. I believe that not only will we see His judgment on America, but on all nations of the world who have continually been warned but ignored His warning. We will see God's wrath being poured out on sin.

As I was in prayer for our nation, I had this feeling that perhaps we too may have reached that point when the cup of iniquity for America is full. And if that is true, then we are now going to experience God's wrath.

I am encouraged by reports of God's blessing and of people coming to the Lord. Perhaps we, too, can have a reprieve from it as happened in Josiah's time. There is one thing that we can be confident in, and that is that right up until the time of judgment, His messengers will continue to warn us.

Judah Ignored God's Repeated Call to Repent

This is what the Lord says: I am going to bring disaster on this place and its people... because they have forsaken me ...and aroused my anger. ... My anger will be poured out on this place and will not be quenched.

2 Chronicles 34:24–25

I believe the time has come when God will pour out His anger on the sin of America and her people. If we confess our sin, repent of our waywardness, and turn to Him, we will receive pardon and forgiveness, but if we do not, we will experience His wrath. "Whoever conceals their sins does not prosper, but the one who confesses and renounces them finds mercy" (Proverbs 28:13). Judgment will always fall on those who do not repent of their sins, and sometimes even on those who do, as we saw in the time of Josiah.

God started out human existence with the warning that judgment will fall on those who sin. It is an eternal principle:

judgment comes upon the sinner. Mankind failed at this point in the garden, and we are still not getting it. When God's judgment does fall on mankind, they blame God for it.

Judgment Will Fall on People and Nations

"I am going to bring disaster on this place and its people. ...Because they have forsaken me and aroused my anger" (2 Chronicles 34:24–25).

The Lord did not turn away from the heat of his fierce anger, which burned against Judah because of all that Manasseh had done to arouse his anger. So the Lord said, "I will remove Judah also from my presence as I removed Israel, and I will reject Jerusalem, the city I chose, and this temple, about which I said, 'My name shall be there.'"

2 Kings 23:26–27

We are not on a brownie point system where our good deeds outweigh our bad deeds. We will either obey God's commands and enjoy His divine approval, or we will disobey and incur His wrath. Our nation is not any better than Israel and Judah. Just as they experienced God's wrath for their sin, so we will too. God is no respecter of people. He does not play favorites with anyone. Whenever there is sin, He exposes it and deals with it through judgment, or, if it has been confessed and repented of, He will forgive and heal.

God not only pours out His wrath against people, but He also pours out His wrath upon nations. Over and over, we see this in God's dealing with Israel in the Old Testament. God raises up nations, and He puts them down. In Proverbs, it says, "Blessed is the nation whose God is the Lord."

Corruption as God Sees It

> *Now the earth was corrupt in God's sight and was full of violence. God saw how corrupt the earth had become, for all the people on earth had corrupted their ways. So God said to Noah, "I am going to put an end to all people, for the earth is filled with violence because of them. I am surely going to destroy both them and the earth."*

Genesis 6:11–13

The Bible says, "The earth was corrupt in God's sight" (Genesis 6:11). It is corruption as God sees it, not the way humans see it. This is the standard set by God, not man. It is His standard of holiness and righteousness. Mankind, in his sinful condition, cannot understand God's sense of holiness. Mankind seems to always explain away or make excuses for their sin, or we compare our sin that, in our eyes, is not as bad as another's and justify ourselves. We must see sin as God sees it, for that is the basis by which we will be judged. To do that, we must become people of the Word of God. Read it! Know it! Learn it! Live it!

> *The person without the Spirit does not accept the things that come from the Spirit of God but considers them foolishness, and he cannot understand them because they are discerned only through the Spirit.*

1 Corinthians 2:14

Mankind is incapable of discerning or understanding spiritual truth without the Holy Spirit.

God's Wrath Cannot and Will Not Be Stopped

> *"My anger will be poured out on this place and will not be quenched" (2 Kings 22:16–17).*

This is what the Lord says: I am going to bring disaster on this place and its people, according to everything written in the book the king of Judah has read. Because they have forsaken me and burned incense to other gods and aroused my anger by all the idols their hands have made, my anger will burn against this place and will not be quenched.

2 Kings 22:16–17

When mankind crosses the line of the "fullness of the wrath of God," God says, "I will do it!" And He will!

Sodom and Gomorrah Are Examples

God's Inquiry

The Lord said,

The outcry against Sodom and Gomorrah is so great and their sin so grievous that I will go down and see if what they have done is as bad as the outcry that has reached me. If not, I will know.

Genesis 18:20–21

God could not find even ten people who were righteous in Sodom and Gomorrah

God's Warning

"We are going to destroy this place. The outcry to the Lord against its people is so great that he has sent us to destroy it" (Genesis 19:13).

God's Judgment

Then the Lord rained down burning sulfur on Sodom and Gomorrah—from the Lord out of the heavens. Thus he overthrew those cities and the

entire plain, destroying all those living in the cities—and also the vegetation in the land.

Genesis 19:24–25

God's Judgment Will Also Fall on the US because of Sin

We are no different than other nations that God has dealt with. Just as God judged them for their sin, He will judge us for our sin. He will deal with us just as He did with these wicked cities. God has not changed. His standard of righteousness still prevails, and He will judge accordingly. As our nation continues down this path of sin, Christians need to be prepared for some hard times spiritually, politically, economically, and physically (the natural realm). We are beginning even now to see these things happen!

God Will Warn the US through His Servants

God Had His Messengers Then, and He Has Them Now

When the king heard the words of the Law, he tore his robes. ..."Go inquire of the Lord for me and for the remnant in Israel and Judah about what is written in this book that has been found. Great is the Lord's anger that is poured out on us because those who have gone before us have not kept the word of the Lord; they have not acted in accordance with all that is written in this book." Hilkiah and those the king sent with him went to speak to the prophetess Huldah. ...She said to them, "This is what the Lord, the God of Israel, says: ...I am going to bring disaster on this place and its people—all the curses written in the book ...because they have forsaken me."

2 Chronicles 34:19, 21–25

Then the king called together all the elders of Judah and Jerusalem. He went up to the temple of

> *the Lord with the people of Judah, the inhabitants*
> *of Jerusalem, the priests and the Levites—all the*
> *people from the least to the greatest. He read in*
> *their hearing all the words of the Book of the*
> *Covenant, which had been found in the temple of*
> *the Lord.*
>
> **2 Chronicles 34:29–30**

God will always have those through whom He speaks to His people. He is faithful to warn both the world and His church. The warning will be given to the people. God has those through whom He is warning us today of His coming judgment.

This warning was so severe that King Josiah felt that everyone should know and be aware of what was about to happen. When King Josiah was given the message from Huldah, he immediately called all of the leaders of the people from both the priesthood as well as his cabinet and shared with them the warning given by the prophetess Huldah. And we, too, must be just as diligent in our concern for those around us and warn them of the coming catastrophe.

Regrettably, Not Everyone Will Hear

Sadly, Scripture is full of examples of people who chose not to heed God's warning:

Noah and the flood: the people would not hear or heed God's warning until it was too late. God had already shut the door to the ark, and their only hope of escape was gone. The Bible says that there were only eight people who escaped, Noah, his wife, and their three sons, and their wives.

Jeremiah and Judah: Jeremiah warned the people and the king about the coming judgment; for his message, Jeremiah was arrested and thrown in a pit. But the message came true,

247

just as he had told them.

Hosea serves as an illustration to Israel: God used Hosea as a living example to demonstrate to Israel how He was dealing with them. He had Hosea marry a prostitute; then, when she left Hosea, God sent him after her to bring her back time and time again. Through this relationship, God illustrated to Israel how He was continuing to reach out to them and bring them back to Himself. Sadly, they refused to give heed to Hosea's message, and as a result, they suffered for it.

Jonah and Nineveh: When God sent Jonah to warn Nineveh of the coming judgment, they heard the warning and heeded the message and repented, and as a result, they were saved.

Samuel: When Israel asked Samuel for a king, Samuel cried to the Lord, but God said to him, "It is not you they have rejected, but they have rejected me as their king" (1 Samuel 8:6–7).

Josiah's message to his people: When Josiah read the words of the Book of the Law to the people, they committed themselves to serve God. As long as Josiah lived, they were true to the Lord.

People are the same today, some will hear and heed the warning, and others will choose not to heed it.

"This Is What the Lord Says!"

May godly men and women be raised up as messengers who will tell us what the Word of the Lord is! Men and women who have been alone with God and have heard from Him and can say, "This is the Word of the Lord." And may God open the hearts and minds of the people to receive His Word.

There Are Those Who Will Hear God's Word

The People Heard and Renewed the Covenant

The King Heard

The king stood by his pillar and renewed the covenant in the presence of the Lord—to follow the Lord and keep his commandments, statutes and decrees with his heart and all his soul, and to obey the words of the covenant written in the book.

2 Chronicles 34:31

The People Heard

"Then he had everyone in Jerusalem and Benjamin pledge themselves to it; the people of Jerusalem did this in accordance with the covenant of God, the God of their ancestors" (2 Chronicles 34:32).

The People Acted on What They Had Heard

Josiah removed all the detestable idols from all the territory belonging to the Israelites, and he had all who were present in Israel serve the Lord their God. As long as he lived, they did not fail to follow the Lord, the God of their ancestors.

2 Chronicles 34:33

They Celebrated the Passover

"Josiah celebrated the Passover to the Lord in Jerusalem, and the Passover lamb was slaughtered on the fourteenth day of the month" (2 Chronicles 35:1).

In Jonah's day, the city of Nineveh repented and turned from its evil ways (Jonah 3:10). When God saw what they did and how they turned from their evil ways, He had compassion and did not bring upon them the destruction He had threatened.

The Response

Because your heart was responsive and you humbled yourself before God when you heard

> *what he spoke against this place and its people,*
> *and because you humbled yourself before me and*
> *tore your robes and wept in my presence, I have*
> *heard you, declares the Lord.*

> **2 Chronicles 34:27**

Look at the response from Josiah:

The king humbled himself.

The king tore his robes.

The king wept before the Lord.

The king removed the detestable idols.

There was real repentance and sorrow for sin. Wherever there is true repentance for sin, there you will find God's mercy and grace. He will do the same for us today if we will humble ourselves, turn from our wicked ways, and serve Him.

There Are Those Whose Hearts Will Respond to God's Word

There are still those today who want to know the truth, and they will respond to the Word of the Lord. The Holy Spirit is still faithful to convict of sin and draw men and women to Himself.

> *Anyone who believes in him will never be put to*
> *shame. For there is no difference between Jew and*
> *Gentile—the same Lord is Lord of all and richly*
> *blesses all who call on him, for, "Everyone who*
> *calls on the name of the Lord will be saved."*
> *How, then, can they call on the one they have not*
> *believed in? And how can they believe in the one of*
> *whom they have not heard? And how can they hear*
> *without someone preaching to them? And how can*
> *they preach unless they are sent? As it is written,*

"How beautiful are the feet of those who bring good news!"

Romans 10:11–15

There are those who, when the message is given to them, will humble themselves, repent and turn to the Lord in true sorrow for their sin.

CHAPTER THIRTEEN:
America on the Brink (Part 2)

God's Wrath May Be Delayed

If my people, who are called by my name, will humble themselves and pray and seek my face and turn from their wicked ways, then will I hear from heaven, and will forgive their sin and heal their land.

2 Chronicles 7:14

Introduction

God pronounced judgment on the nation of Judah because of her continued sin in the face of God's call to repent, but God pronounced a delay of His judgment upon Judah because of the repentant heart of Josiah. In this chapter, we will examine why the delay and the purpose of the delay.

God's Judgment May Be Delayed

We Must Realize Our Sin

Great is the Lord's anger that burns against us because those who have gone before us have not obeyed the words of this book; they have not acted in accordance with all that is written there concerning us.

2 Kings 22:13

Great is the Lord's anger that is poured out on us because those who have gone before us have not kept the word of the Lord; they have not acted in accordance with all that is written in this book.

2 Chronicles 34:21

Before there can be a delay in God's wrath, the people must recognize their sin and repent of it. Josiah realized the greatness of their sin and repented before the Lord. Then he read the Word to the people, and when confronted with their sin, they, too, repented.

If America is to receive mercy from the Lord, she too must realize her sin and repent. We, like Judah, are on the brink of the outpouring of God's wrath upon us. Then we must confess our sin to the Lord. If we do, He is merciful and will hear and pardon us.

We Must Realize the Sins of Our Parents

"Great is the Lord's anger that burns against us because those who have gone before us have not acted in accordance with all that is written there" (2 Kings 22:13).

"Great is the Lord's anger that is poured out on us because those who have gone before us have not

kept the word of the Lord" (2 Chronicles 34:21).

Josiah realized that they were going to experience God's wrath because their parents before them failed to heed God's Word and obey it. Most of the kings were wicked because their fathers before them were wicked. Parents set the example for their children. Parents pass on to their children their values and character through the way they live. Children watch what their parents do, and it affects the way they will live their lives. May God give us godly parents who will teach and instruct their children in righteousness.

Righteousness, too, is passed on to your children from generation to generation. Scripture declares that God will bless to one thousand generations those who will obey His Word (Exodus 20:5–6). The legacy you leave will follow you into the next generation.

We Cannot Repent of Something We Don't Recognize as Sin

It is too easy to justify what we do not recognize as sin. From the time children are little, they must be taught what is right and what is wrong. If sin has been a way of life, you probably won't see it as sin. It is important to know and understand God's standard of righteousness. Only then will people know what sin is and what is not. Instruction and discipleship must be part of the ministry of the church so they will comprehend God's standard of holiness.

The Delay Is Caused by True Repentance

King Josiah Truly Repented

> *Because your heart was responsive and you humbled yourself before the Lord when you heard what I have spoken against this place and its people—that they would become a curse and be*

laid to waste—and because you tore your robes and wept in my presence, I also have heard you, declares the Lord.

2 Kings 22:19

Because your heart was responsive and you humbled yourself before God when you heard what he spoke against this place and its people, and because you humbled yourself before me and tore your robes and wept in my presence, I have heard you, declares the Lord.

2 Chronicles 34:27

Josiah displayed true sorrow for sin:

1. He heard the Word of the Lord,

2. He believed the Word of the Lord,

3. He took the Word for himself—"I am a sinner,"

4. He humbled himself before God,

5. He tore his clothe and wept before the Lord.

Josiah had true sorrow for sin. He displayed authentic remorse for the sin of his people and his fathers. He also realized that *their* sin was *his* sin. He didn't try to excuse himself but acknowledged that he, too, must repent.

Only True Repentance Will Delay God's Judgment

If my people, who are called by my name, will humble themselves and pray, and seek my face and turn from their wicked ways, then will hear from heaven, and will forgive their sin and will heal their land.

2 Chronicles 7:14

God has placed some requirements on the delay of judgment. It is conditional:

1. If My people (only *if* they will humble themselves),
2. Those called by His name,
3. Will humble themselves before Him,
4. Will pray and seek His face and His will,
5. And turn from their wicked ways (complete turning from, and forsaking, of sin).

Without true repentance, there will be no delay in God's judgment. It is based on the condition of genuine repentance and turning from sin.

God Will Hear, Forgive Their Sin, and Delay His Judgment.

> *"I have heard you, declares the Lord"* (2 Chronicles 34:27).

> *"Then will I hear from heaven, and forgive and heal"* (2 Chronicles 7:14).

The Word of the Lord to Josiah was that it was to be a delay because of his repentance, but God's judgment would be poured out at a future time. Their sin had become so great that it must be punished. The delay would be because of their turning to God, but it would not stop the impending judgment!

The Delay Is so Others May Hear and Repent

God Wants All to Repent

> *"Not wanting anyone to perish, but everyone to come to repentance"* (2 Peter 3:9).

We must understand the heart of God. He gave Himself for all mankind. His plan was for all of mankind to accept

His Son as their Savior and join with Him in heaven for all eternity. No one needs to perish or be lost! The tragedy of hell is that those who will go there do not have to.

> *"This gospel of the kingdom will be preached in the whole world as a testimony to all nations, and then the end will come" (Matthew 24:14).*

The purpose of the "Great Commission" is that "everyone who calls on the name of the Lord will be saved" (Romans 10:13).

The People Repented and Made a Covenant with God

> *Then he [Josiah] had everyone in Jerusalem and Benjamin pledge themselves to it; the people of Jerusalem did this in accordance with the covenant of God, the God of their ancestors. ...As long as he [Josiah] lived, they did not fail to follow the Lord, the God of their ancestors.*

2 Chronicles 34:32–33

This Is a One-Time Commitment for the Rest of Your Life

> *"As long as he lived, they did not fail to follow the Lord, the God of their ancestors" (2 Chronicles 34:33).*

The people sincerely committed themselves to God, and He rewarded them by delaying His judgment. Choosing to obey God's Word is to be a life-long commitment. This is not something done out of convenience or because we feel good about it at the time; no, it was to be permanent. On God's part, it is to be for eternity. Nor is it just for our personal advantage. If we only serve when it is to our personal advantage to follow Christ, then when it is not, we think we don't have to. God will keep His committed to us for eternity.

The Church Will Be God's Witnessing Team

Josiah Was Compelled to Proclaim the Message

Then the king called together all the elders of Judah and Jerusalem. He went up to the temple of the Lord with the people of Judah, the inhabitants of Jerusalem, the priests and the Levites—all the people from the least to the greatest. He read in their hearing all the words of the Book of the Covenant.

2 Chronicles 34:29–30

Josiah read to them all the words of the Book of the Law. He did not pick and choose what to read; he read it all to them. He did not edit it, and he did not dilute it; he presented God's Word just as it was; what God called sin, he called sin.

Just as Josiah felt compelled to share what he found with others so we, too, must feel compelled to share. We are not only responsible for ourselves, but we are responsible for sharing God's message with others as well. May God help us to go forth boldly and proclaim His good news.

People Cannot Repent if They Don't Know

How, then, can they call on the one they have not believed in? And how can they believe in the one of whom they have not heard? And how can they hear without someone preaching to them? And how can they preach unless they are sent?

Romans 10:14–15

Faith comes from hearing the message, and the message is heard through the Word of Christ. We are not responsible for their decision, but we are responsible for giving them the gospel so they can come to a point of decision.

> *"This gospel ... will be preached in the whole world ... and then the end" (Matthew 24:14).*

> *"He [Jesus] said to them, 'Go into the whole world and preach the gospel to all creation" (Mark 16:15).*

We cannot forget what God's people are here for—the proclamation of the gospel. We are not here for our own benefit but to share the good news with those He puts us in contact with. Our time for indulgence will come when we are in His presence. Many believers spend their time acquiring *things* when He has promised us that He will take care of everything we need. We must not get sidetracked with the things of this life. Rather we must be about our Father's business.

Common Concerns of the World Today

In most of the nations of the world, the greatest concerns include:

1. Daily food,

2. Famine,

3. Sickness and disease,

4. The basic necessities of life.

The greatest concern for Americans is the loss of our wealth. May God help us to get our priorities in the right order!

The Church Will Minister in Power and Glory

The Gospel Is Proclaimed

"Josiah read in their [the people] hearing all the words of the Book of the Covenant" (2 Chronicles 34:30).

The church is never as powerful as when the gospel is preached. The church is at its best when we preach Jesus. We must proclaim Him. He is the gospel! We must proclaim Him boldly to all who will listen. Don't be ashamed to present Him wherever you are. Proclaim Him to your neighbors, in the store, at the gas station, in the bank, on the job, wherever you are. As the hymn says, "We have a story to tell the nations, a story of truth and life." Paul said,

> *I am obligated both to the Greeks and non-Greeks, both to the wise and the foolish. That is why I am so eager to preach ... also to you. For I am not ashamed of the gospel because it is the power of God that brings salvation to everyone who believes.*
>
> **Romans 1:14–16**

May we have that same eagerness and excitement about this great news.

The People Will Live for God

"As long as he [Josiah] lived, they did not fail to follow the Lord, the God of their ancestors" (2 Chronicles 34:33).

As a result of following the Lord, His people will reap all of the good things which follow a life of righteousness. No divorce, nor heartache from broken homes and families.

No immorality and resulting sickness and disease. No more AIDS! No drugs or alcohol nor the tragedies of drug abuse. People will get along with each other and have a genuine love for others. No crime, murder, thievery, envy, strife; no lying, cheating, abusive behavior, or any of the heartaches and sorrow that go with that kind of conduct.

The Church Will Display the Power of God

Josiah took a stand against all ungodliness. He went throughout the land and destroyed the idols and the altars to heathen gods. He didn't do it secretly but boldly took a stand against idolatry.

People must know where we stand. Those in our community will know that we in the Church know and obey God's Word. The church must know how to pray. People will come to us for prayer because they know we will pray for them. The church will go forth in God's might, and those around us will see Christ in us.

Christians will walk in power and authority: The sick will be healed, the lame will walk, the blind will see, the disease will disappear, and the miraculous will accompany the ministry of the gospel. It will happen as Jesus said, "Go into all the world and preach the good news to all creation." And these signs will accompany those who believe:

> *In my name they will drive out demons; they will speak in new tongues; they will pick up snakes with their hands; and when they drink deadly poison, it will not hurt them a all; they will place their hands on sick people, and they will be well.*

Mark 16:17–18

People of the world will call upon the church for help and prayer. As long as we remain humble as Josiah did, we will see a great harvest and be part of His ministry team.

There Will Be a Price to Pay

Not everyone will hear and respond to the gospel. Christians will be blamed for the problems facing our country. They could be mocked and ridiculed and even persecuted for the gospel's sake. It may cost you your employment. You may even lose everything you have. But at the same time, you will walk in power and glory in the name of the Lord. Put on the whole armor of God and go forth in victory. God will provide miraculously for your needs. There will be those who will see God at work through you and come to Him. "A servant is not greater than his master. If they persecuted me, they will persecute you also. ...They will treat you this way because of my name" (John 15:20–21).

Conclusion

If we humble ourselves and pray, seek His face, turn from our wicked ways, then I believe we will be granted a delay in the coming judgment. During that delay, it will be a time of great harvest for the kingdom as the church ministers in power and glory. But it will only happen if we do as Josiah did and seek the Lord.

A brief summary of how God's wrath may be delayed:

1. God's Judgment May Be Delayed

2. The Delay of Judgment Is because of True Repentance

3. The Delay Will Be so Others Can Hear and Repent

4. We Are to Be Part of God's Witnessing Team

5. The Church Will Be Filled with the Power and Glory of God

Appendix

Chronology of Josiah's Life

About 931 BC: The "man of God" predicted the destruction of King Jeroboam's altar at Bethel by Josiah 350 years before Josiah's birth (1 Kings 13:1–32).

726–697 BC: Hezekiah, a godly king, Josiah's great grandfather, became king of Judah at age twenty-five and reigned for twenty-nine years (2 Kings 18:1–2; 2 Chronicles 29:1).

697–641 BC: Manasseh, Josiah's grandfather, became king of Judah at age twelve and reigned for fifty-five years (2 Kings 21:1; 2 Chronicles 33:1). (Because of his ungodly reign, God would send Judah into seventy years of captivity into Babylon.)

641–639 BC: Amon, Josiah's father, became king at age twenty-two and reigned for two years and was murdered by his own officers (2 Kings 21:18b–19; 2 Chronicles 34:21).

642–630 BC: Nahum, the prophet, prophesied during Amon's reign and the first part of Josiah's (2 Kings 21–24; 2 Chronicles 33–36).

648 BC: Josiah was born to Amon at age sixteen (2 Kings 22:1; 2 Chronicles 34:1).

639 BC: Amon was assassinated by his own servants at age twenty-four after reigning just two years (2 Kings 21:23, 26a; 2 Chronicles 34:21).

639–608 BC: Josiah became king at age eight (2 Kings 21:24–

25; 2 Chronicles 34:3).

About 632 BC: Zephaniah, the prophet, a contemporary and relative of Josiah, prophesied during his reign (Zephaniah 1:1; 2 Kings 22–24; 2 Chronicles 34–36).

633 BC: In Josiah's sixth year as king, his first child, Johanan, is born at age fourteen (1 Chronicles 3:15; 2 Kings 23:36; 2 Chronicles 36:5).

631 BC: In his eighth year as king, he begins to seek the Lord at age sixteen (2 Chronicles 34:3).

627 BC: In his twelfth year as king, he began to purge Judah and Jerusalem of heathen idols at age twenty (2 Chronicles 34:3–7).

628 BC: In his thirteenth year as king, Jeremiah began his prophetic ministry (Jeremiah 1:2).

621 BC: In his eighteenth year as king at age twenty-six, his last child, Jehoiachin (Zedekiah), was born (2 Kings 24:18; 2 Chronicles 36:11).

621 BC: In his eighteenth year as king, he repaired the temple of the Lord at age twenty-six (2 Kings 22:3–7; 2 Chronicles 34:8–13).

621 BC: In his eighteenth year as king, the Book of the Law was found and read to him. Josiah is alarmed at what he hears (2 Kings 22:8–10; 2 Chronicles 34:14–15).

621 BC: A delegation was sent to Huldah, the prophetess, at age twenty-six (2 Kings 22:12–20; 2 Chronicles 34:16–28). Because Josiah turned to the Lord, the captivity would not come during his reign (2 Chronicles 34:16–28).

621 BC: Josiah had the Book of the Law read to the people (2 Kings 23:1–2; 2 Chronicles 34:29–30).

621 BC: King Josiah made a covenant with God to follow the

Lord and keep His commands, regulations, and decrees with all his heart and all his soul, thus confirming the words of the covenant written in the book. Then all the people pledged themselves to the covenant (2 Kings 23:3; 2 Chronicles 34:31–32).

621–620 BC: Josiah made further reformations, both in Judah and in Israel (2 Kings 23:4–14, 24; 2 Chronicles 34:33).

About 622–620 BC: The fulfillment of the prophecy of the "man of God" to destroy the altar made 350 years earlier (2 Kings 23:15–20; 2 Chronicles 34:6–7).

621 BC: Josiah had Israel and Judah celebrate the Passover in the eighteenth year of his reign (2 Kings 23:21–23; 2 Chronicles 35:1–19).

About 612–598 BC: Habakkuk, the prophet, ministered during the last part of Josiah's reign and into Jehoiakim's reign (2 Kings 23–25; 2 Chronicles 36).

608 BC: In the thirty-first year of his reign, King Josiah fought against Necho, king of Egypt, and was killed in battle. He was thirty-nine (2 Kings 23:28–30a; 2 Chronicles 35:20–25).

608 BC: Jehoahaz, Josiah's son, was made king at age twenty-three. He reigned for three months and was taken captive by King Necho to Egypt and died there (2 Kings 23:30b–31; 2 Chronicles 36:1–2). He did that which was evil in the sight of the Lord (2 Kings 23:32).

608–597 BC: Pharaoh Necho made Josiah's son, Eliakim (also known as Jehoiakim), king in place of his brother. He was twenty-five years old when he began his reign and reigned for eleven years (2 Kings 23:36; 2 Chronicles 36:5). He did that which was evil in the sight of the Lord (2 Kings 23:37; 2 Chronicles 36:5).

597 BC: Jehoiachin, Jehoiakim's son, was made king. He was eighteen years old and reigned for three months (2 Kings 24:8; 2 Chronicles 36:9). He was taken captive to Babylon and remained there until his death (2 Kings 24:10–12; 2 Kings 25:27–30). He did that which was evil in the sight of the Lord (2 Kings 24:19; 2 Chronicles 36:9).

597–586 BC: Zedekiah, Josiah's third son, was placed on the throne by Nebuchadnezzar. He was twenty-one years old and reigned eleven years (2 Kings 24:18; 2 Chronicles 36:11).

586 BC: Zedekiah rebelled and was taken captive to Babylon. His children were murdered before his eyes, and then they put his eyes out (2 Kings 25:3–7). He did that which was evil in the sight of the Lord (2 Kings 24:19; 2 Chronicles 36:12).

586 BC: Jerusalem was captured by Babylon.

586 BC: Jerusalem was captured by Babylon and the temple was destroyed.

Bibliography

Blaikie, William G. *A Manual of Bible History*. New York: The Ronald Press Co, 1940.

Crockett, William Day. *A Harmony of Samuel, Kings, and Chronicles*. Baker Book House, 1951.

Halley, Henry H. *Halley's Bible Handbook*. 24th ed. Grand Rapids, Michigan: Zondervan Publishing House, 1965.

Henry, Matthew. *Matthew Henry's Commentary on the Whole Bible*. 2. Vol. 2. 6 vols. Fleming H. Revell Co., n.d.

Josephus, Flavius. *The Life and Works of Flavius Josephus*. Translated by William Whiston A. M. Holt, Rinehart and Winston, 1957.

Lockyer, Herbert. *All the Men of the Bible*. Grand Rapids, Michigan: Zondervan, Publishing House, 1958

Maclaren, Alexander. *Expositions of Holy Scripture*. 3. Vol. 3. Eerdmans Publishing Co., n.d.

Maclear, G. F. *A Class-Book of Old Testament History*. Grand Rapids, Michigan: Eerdmans Publishing Co., n.d.

Bromiley, Geoffrey W. *The International Standard Bible Encyclopedia*. 3. Vol. 3. Eerdmans, 1995.

Pusey, Edward B. *The Minor Prophets: With a Commentary, Explanatory and Practical, and Introductions to the Several Books*. 1. Vol. 1. Michigan: Baker Book House Grand Rapids, 1860.

Scroggie, Graham W. *Know Your Bible*. 1. Vol. 1. London: Pickering & Inglis Ltd, 1965.

Smith, James, and Robert Lee. *Handfuls on Purpose: For*

Christian Workers and Bible Students. 6. Vol. 6. 12 vols. London: Pickering & Inglis, n.d.

Spence, Rev. H.D. M. DD and Exell, Rev. Joseph S. MA, *The Pulpit Commentary, Volumes 11, 12, 14,* Wilcox & Follett Co. Publishers & Funk & Wagnalls Co. London and New York.

Tenney, Merrill C. General Editor, *The Zondervan Pictorial Encyclopedia of the Bible, Vols. First-5,* Zondervan Publishing House Grand Rapids, Michigan, 1975.

Horton, Stanley M. *Adult Teacher: The Word of Life Series of Adult Bible Lessons Based on Outlines From the Evangelical Curriculum Commission.* 3. Vol. 3. Springfield, Missouri: Gospel Publishing House, 1980.

About the Author

J. Paul Taylor was born and raised in Tacoma, Washington. He is a graduate of Northwest University in Kirkland, Washington, and has been ordained with the Assemblies of God for fifty-seven years. He spent forty-six years in pastoral ministry.

God gave him a heart for missions, and the churches he pastored gave over twenty percent of their income to missions. He has had the privilege of ministering in seven nations overseas.

Paul and his wife, Dawn, have been married for over sixty-five years. They dedicated each one of their six children to the Lord and to His service. God took them at their word, and all their children are in ministry, some here in the US and some overseas. And those who are not in full-time ministry are involved in their local church ministries.

Paul and Dawn have fifteen grandchildren and twelve great-grandchildren and are living in Gig Harbor, Washington.